Wonders

Mc
Graw
Hill
Education

www.mheonline.com/readingwonders

Send all inquiries to:
McGraw-Hill Education
2 Penn Plaza
New York, New York 10121

ISBN: 978-0-02-131134-7
MHID: 0-02-131134-X

Printed in the United States of America.

3 4 5 6 7 8 9 QVS 20 19 18 17 16   B

California

Wonders

ELD
My Language Book

Program Authors

Diane August

Jana Echevarria

Josefina V. Tinajero

Mc
Graw
Hill
Education

Unit 1

Unit 3

Unit 4

Unit 5

Unit Opener: Wonders of Nature

Unit 6

Unit 7

Unit 8

Unit 9   Unit Opener: **How Things Change** 208

Unit 10

Unit Opener: Thinking Outside the Box ... 234

Unit 1
Take a New Step

The Big Idea

What can we learn when we try new things?

? Essential Question

How can we get along with new friends?

COLLABORATE

Weekly Concept: Make New Friends Guide children to talk about the picture. Ask: *What are the two children doing on the floor? Who wants to play with them? Draw something the three friends could play with together.*

Ask partners to imagine what the children in the picture are saying, and share their ideas. Invite groups to act out the scene. See Teacher's Edition p. 6 for scaffolded support with this page.

COLLABORATE

Words and Categories: Identify Feelings Guide children to use a feeling word to describe each face (e.g. tired, happy, surprised, silly, mad, scared). Have children draw in the missing faces.

Ask partners to use a feeling word and an action to complete this sentence frame: *I feel _____ so I _____ .* (E.g. *I feel happy so I smile.*) See Teacher's Edition p. 9 for scaffolded support with this page.

Respond to the Text: *What About Bear?* Review the book, then ask children to name the characters. Ask: *Which animals played together first? Circle their pictures. What problem did the animals have?* Then ask children to draw the three animals playing together.

Invite partners to work together to retell the story. Then have them share their favorite ways to play using this sentence frame: *I like to _____ with my friends.* See Teacher's Edition p. 12 for scaffolded support with this page.

ELD.PI.K.6.Em, ELD.PI.K.6.Ex, ELD.PI.K.6.Br; ELD.PI.K.12a.Em, ELD.PI.K.12a.Ex, ELD.PI.K.12a.Br See the California Standards section

COLLABORATE

Oral Vocabulary: Match Feelings and Causes Guide children to describe the pictures, naming the feelings shown on the children's *faces.* Have them draw a line to match the feeling shown on each *child's* face with the object that is likely to cause that feeling.

Ask partners to tell about a time they experienced each of the feelings shown, and share what caused them to feel that way. Offer a sentence frame: *I felt _____ because _____ .* See Teacher's Edition p. 16 for scaffolded support with this page.

1.

2.

3.

4.

Retell: "I Can" Review the selection, then ask children to retell it using complete sentences. Prompt them with questions such as: *What does the boy see? What does he say?* Offer sentence frames: *The boy can see ____ . The boy says ____ .*

Ask partners to look around the room and use this sentence frame to name what they see: *I can see the _____.* See Teacher's Edition p. 18 for scaffolded support with this page.

ELD.PI.K.6.Em, ELD.PI.K.6.Ex, ELD.PI.K.6.Br; ELD.PI.K.12a.Em, ELD.PI.K.12a.Ex, ELD.PI.K.12a.Br See the California Standards section

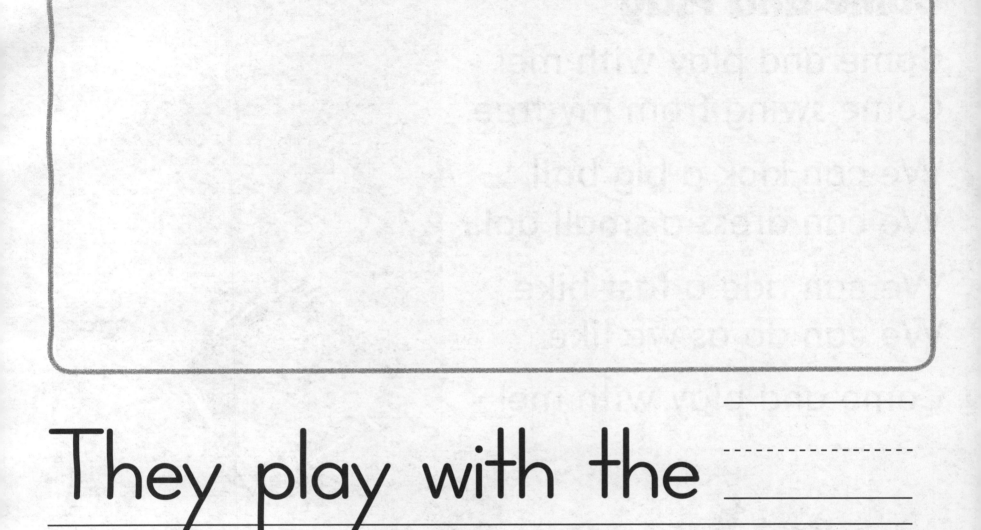

They play with the _____

_____

_____ .

Writing Review "I Can" with children. Remind them of the writing prompt: *How can the boy and a friend play with the things in the story?* Guide children to draw the boy and a friend playing with one thing from the text, and complete the sentence.

COLLABORATE

Ask partners to share their drawing and writing. Then have them choose one object from the book, and make a list of different ways that two friends can play with it. See Teacher's Edition p. 19 for scaffolded support with this page.

Come and Play

Come and play with me!
Come swing from my tree.

We can kick a big ball.
We can dress a small doll.

We can ride a fast bike.
We can do as we like.

Come and play with me!

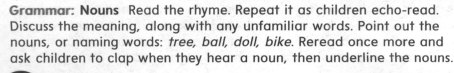

Grammar: Nouns Read the rhyme. Repeat it as children echo-read. Discuss the meaning, along with any unfamiliar words. Point out the nouns, or naming words: *tree, ball, doll, bike*. Reread once more and ask children to clap when they hear a noun, then underline the nouns.

Ask partners to create a line to replace *We can kick a big ball*, such as *We can push a red truck* or *We can read a good book*. Help children identify the nouns in the new lines. See Teacher's Edition p. 25 for scaffolded support with this page.

ELD.PI.K.5.Em, ELD.PI.K.5.Ex, ELD.PI.K.5.Br; ELD.PII.K.4.Em
See the California Standards section

1.

the
paper

2.

the ✂
scissors

3.

the 🧶
string

4.

the
kite

Fluency Track the words and read the story aloud as children echo-read, copying your pronunciation. Talk about what happens in the story. Then have students read it on their own, and circle the high-frequency word *the*.

Ask partners to take turns reading the story to each other until they can read it fluently. Then have them tell the story in their own words, using the vocabulary words shown in the story. See Teacher's Edition p. 26 for scaffolded support with this page.

ELD.PI.K.5.Em, ELD.PI.K.5.Ex, ELD.PI.K.5.Br; ELD.PIII.K
See the California Standards section

Weekly Concept: Get Up and Go!

? Essential Question
How do baby animals move?

Weekly Concept **Get up and Go!** Guide children to talk about the picture. Ask them to use words and gestures to describe how each type of animal moves. Have children add to the picture by drawing another baby animal, then describe that animal's movement.

Have partners play animal charades: one partner acts out an animal movement and the other partner tries to name both the animal and the movement (e.g. *a rabbit hops*). See Teacher's Edition p. 30 for scaffolded support with this page.

Words and Categories: **Number Words** Guide children to count the fingers shown in the top row, and say the numbers. Have them draw the correct number of bees or spiders in each column to *complete* the page.

COLLABORATE

Invite partners to play a game using number words. One child points to a picture and says: *I see bees. How many do I see?* The other partner responds: *You see _____ bees.* See Teacher's Edition p. 33 for scaffolded support with this page.

ELD.PI.K.I.Em, ELD.PI.K.I.Ex, ELD.PI.K.I.Br See the California Standards section

Unit I • Week 2 • Words and Categories

II

Respond to the Text: *Pouch!* Guide children to name the characters and retell the story. Ask: *What happens after Joey meets the bee? The rabbit? The bird? The baby kangaroo?* Ask children to draw Joey with another character, and label their drawings.

Ask partners to share their work and describe what Joey is doing in their drawings, and how they think he is feeling. See Teacher's Edition p. 36 for scaffolded support with this page.

ELD.PI.K.6.Em, ELD.PI.K.6.Ex, ELD.PI.K.6.Br; ELD.PI.K.I2a.Em, ELD.PI.K.I2a.Ex, ELD.PI.K.I2a.Br; ELD.PII.K.I.Em See the California Standards section

Oral Vocabulary: Animal Movements Guide children to name the animals and describe the different ways they move. Then focus their attention on each row. Ask: *Which two animals in this row move the same way?* Have children circle these animals.

COLLABORATE

Have partners talk about the ways they can move. Then have children ask and answer this question for each animal on this page: *Can you move like a _____?* See Teacher's Edition p. 40 for scaffolded support with this page.

ELD.PI.K.I.Em, ELD.PI.K.I.Ex, ELD.PI.K.I.Br See the California Standards section

1.

2.

3.

4.

Retell: "We Can" Review the story. Then ask the children to retell it from the point of view of the animals, using the sentence frame: *We can* _____ .

COLLABORATE

Ask partners to find ways they both can move, and use sentences to describe them: *We can run, We can jump, We can climb*, etc. See Teacher's Edition p. 42 for scaffolded support with this page.

ELD.PI.K.6.Em, ELD.PI.K.6.Ex, ELD.PI.K.6.Br; ELD.PI.K.I2a.Em, ELD.PI.K.I2a.Ex, ELD.PI.K.I2a.Br See the California Standards section

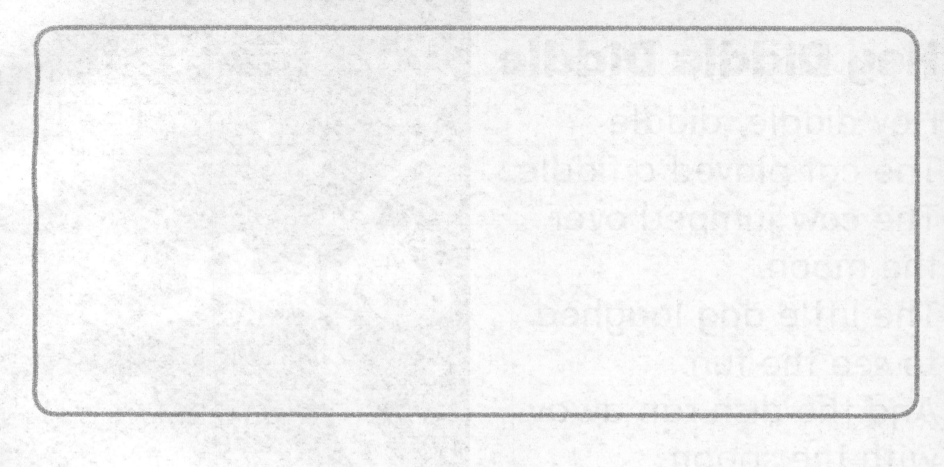

Animals run because

_____

- -

_____ .

COLLABORATE

Writing Review "We Can." Name the types of movement shown. For each, ask: _Why do animals move this way?_ (E.g., They climb to find food/have fun.) Introduce a prompt: _Why do animals run?_ Have children draw an animal and complete the sentence.

Ask partners to share their work, and talk about their pictures. Ask: _What movements can help animals get places? Get food? Escape danger? Play? Cuddle?_ See Teacher's Edition p. 43 for scaffolded support with this page.

ELD.PI.K.6.Em, ELD.PI.K.6.Ex; ELD.PI.K.10.Em, ELD.PI.K.10.Ex
See the California Standards section

Hey Diddle Diddle

Hey diddle, diddle
The cat played a fiddle.
The cow jumped over
the moon.
The little dog laughed
to see the fun.
And the dish ran away
with the spoon.

Grammar: Nouns Read the rhyme, then reread it as children echo-read. Discuss the meaning of each line. Guide children to find the nouns, or naming words. Then ask them to circle the nouns, and match each noun with a part of the illustration.

Ask partners to replace the nouns in one sentence of the rhyme to create a new silly poem. Offer this sentence frame: *The _____ ran away with the _____.* Ask children to list their nouns. See Teacher's Edition p. 49 for scaffolded support with this page.

ELD.PI.K.2.Em; ELD.PI.K.5.Em, ELD.PI.K.5.Ex, ELD.PI.K.5.Br
See the California Standards section

1.

We .

run

2.

We 🐿 .

climb

3.

We 🐱 .

jump

4.

We 🐈 .

sleep

Fluency Track the words as children echo-read the story with you. Remind them to stop and take a breath when they see a period. Have children read the story again, copying your intonation. Then ask them to circle the high-frequency word *we* in each sentence.

ELD.PI.K.5.Em, ELD.PI.K.5.Ex, ELD.PI.K.5.Br; ELD.PI.K.II.Br; ELD.PIII.K See the California Standards section

COLLABORATE

Ask partners to take turns reading the story while the other person echo-reads. Then ask them to offer their opinions on whether they liked the story or not, and to explain why. See Teacher's Edition p. 50 for scaffolded support with this page.

Weekly Concept: Use Your Senses

? Essential Question

How can your senses help you learn?

Weekly Concept: Use Your Senses Guide children to talk about ways people are using their senses in the picture. Ask children to circle each of the following: someone tasting, listening, touching, and smelling.

COLLABORATE

Ask partners to share examples of things they can sense using this frame: *I can _____ a _____,* e.g. *I can taste an apple; I can smell a flower.* See Teacher's Edition p. 54 for scaffolded support with this page.

18 Unit 1 • Week 3 • Weekly Concept

ELD.PI.K.I.Em, ELD.PI.K.I.Ex, ELD.PI.K.I.Br See the California Standards section

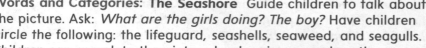

Words and Categories: The Seashore Guide children to talk about the picture. Ask: *What are the girls doing? The boy?* Have children circle the following: the lifeguard, seashells, seaweed, and seagulls. Children can complete the picture by drawing a sand castle.

ELD.PI.K.I.Em, ELD.PI.K.I.Ex, ELD.PI.K.I.Br; ELD.PI.K.3.Em
See the California Standards section

COLLABORATE

Ask partners to imagine they're in the picture, and describe what they see at the beach. Have them offer opinions on the most fun activity on a beach, starting with: *I think _____ is the most fun.* See Teacher's Edition p. 57 for scaffolded support with this page.

COLLABORATE

Respond to the Text: *Senses at the Seashore* Guide children to use the pictures to answer: *What can you see, touch or hear?* Ask children to draw another seashore object and write about what their senses can tell them.

Ask partners to create a "Senses in the Classroom" story, using the sentence pattern provided in the big book, for example: *See the bulletin board. Feel the rug.* See Teacher's Edition p. 60 for scaffolded support with this page.

ELD.PI.K.2.Em, ELD.PI.K.2.Ex; ELD.PI.K.6.Em, ELD.PI.K.6.Ex, ELD.PI.K.6.Br; ELD.PI.K.10.Em See the California Standards section

Unit 2

Let's Explore

The Big Idea

What can you find out when you explore?

Weekly Concept: Tools We Use

? Essential Question

How do tools help us to explore?

Weekly Concept: Tools We Use Guide children to describe the picture. Have them circle and name the tools children are using to explore the nature trail. For each tool ask: *What is the child using? How is the tool helping the child explore?*

Invite partners to pretend they're using tools like the children in the picture, and describe what they're doing. Then have them exchange ideas about other tools the children could use. See Teacher's Edition p. 82 for scaffolded support with this page.

COLLABORATE

Words and Categories: Hand Movements Guide children to describe the action in the each photo, e.g. *digging/scooping, brushing, pulling, picking, pouring*. Then, have students draw themselves using their hands to do a job.

Have partners take turns asking questions about each other's drawings, for the other partner to answer, such as: *What are you doing with your hands? What job are you doing?* See Teacher's Edition p. 85 for scaffolded support with this page.

ELD.PI.K.I.Em, ELD.PI.K.I.Ex, ELD.PI.K.I.Br See the California Standards section

I use a _____ .

Respond to the Text: _The Handiest Things in the World_ Guide children to name the tools and describe how people use them. Ask: _Which tool helps you move dirt/ keep dry/ care for plants?_ Have them draw themselves using a tool, and complete the sentence.

COLLABORATE

Ask partners to describe their pictures and read their sentences to each other. Then invite them to share their experiences using other tools from the Big Book. See Teacher's Edition p. 88 for scaffolded support with this page.

ELD.PI.K.6.Em, ELD.PI.K.6.Ex,ELD.PI.K.6.Br; ELD.PI.K.10.Em
See the California Standards section

COLLABORATE

Oral Vocabulary: Tools Guide children to name and talk about the tools and objects. Have them match each tool with an object.

Ask partners to explain how each tool could help people learn about its matching object. Then have them think of other objects the tools could help people explore. See Teacher's Edition p. 92 for scaffolded support with this page.

1.

2.

3.

4.

Retell: "Pam Can See" Review the story, then ask children to use these pictures to retell it. Ask questions such as: *What can Pam see? What will Pam's mom do with the pot? What objects does Pam choose? What do you think she will do with them?*

COLLABORATE

Invite partners to talk about the kinds of stores that Pam is shopping in, and to name other objects Pam might find in each store. See Teacher's Edition p. 94 for scaffolded support with this page.

ELD.PI.K.6.Em, ELD.PI.K.6.Ex, ELD.PI.K.6.Br; ELD.PI.K.I2a.Em, ELD.PI.K.I2a.Ex, ELD.PI.K.I2a.Br See the California Standards section

The cart _____.

Writing Review "Pam Can See." Introduce the writing prompt: *How is the shopping cart a handy tool for Pam and her mother?* Have children draw how Pam uses the shopping cart. Guide children to complete the sentence to tell how the cart helps Pam.

ELD.PI.K.2.Em; ELD.PI.K.6.Em, ELD.PI.K.6.Ex, ELD.PI.K.6.Br; ELD.PI.K.10.Em, ELD.PI.K.10.Ex See the California Standards section

Ask partners to share their drawing and writing. Then have them list reasons that the shopping cart is a useful tool, such as: *it rolls; it holds a lot; it's strong; it's big,* etc. See Teacher's Edition p. 95 for scaffolded support with this page.

Tools We Use

Scissors cut.

Brushes paint.

Pencils and pens write.

When there is a job to do,
tools help us do it right.

Grammar: Verbs Read the passage. Repeat, having children echo-read. Explain that a verb is an action word, and point out the verbs in the passage. Then read the passage once more, asking children to clap when they hear a verb.

COLLABORATE

Ask partners to act out the meaning of a verb from the passage, then use it in a sentence. E.g. *I cut the paper;* or *I paint a picture.* Then children can do the same thing with new verbs. See Teacher's Edition p. 101 for scaffolded support with this page.

ELD.PI.K.5.Em, ELD.PI.K.5.Ex, ELD.PI.K.5.Br; ELD.PII.K.3a.Em, ELD.PII.K.3a.Ex, ELD.PII.K.3a.Br See the California Standards section

The Map

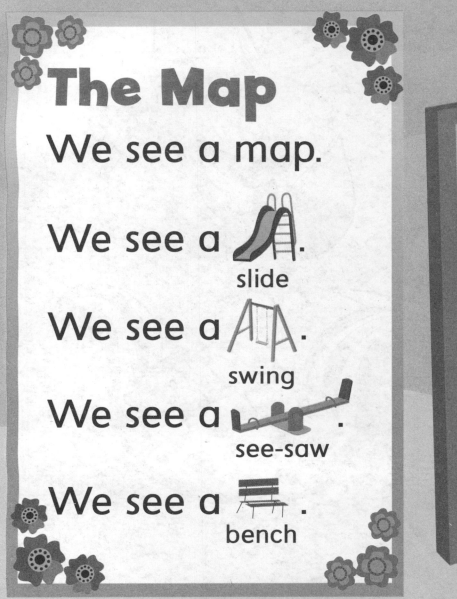

We see a map.

We see a .
slide

We see a _____ .
swing

We see a _____ .
see-saw

We see a _____ .
bench

Fluency Track the words and pictures as children echo-read the passage with you. Then have them read it again, copying your intonation. Ask: *Where are the girl and her mother? What are they doing?* Ask students to underline the high-frequency word *a*.

Ask partners to take turns reading the story to each other until they can read it fluently. Have children search the map for each object in the story, and circle the object when they find it. See Teacher's Edition p. 102 for scaffolded support with this page.

ELD.PI.K.5.Em, ELD.PI.K.5.Ex, ELD.PI.K.5.Br; ELD.PIII.K
See the California Standards section

Weekly Concept: Shapes All Around Us

? Essential Question

What shapes do you see around you?

Weekly Concept: Shapes Guide children to describe the picture, naming both the objects and the shapes. Ask them to circle at least one triangle, rectangle, and square. Then have them mark an "X" on every circle they see, and count how many they can find.

COLLABORATE

Ask partners to take turns naming shapes in the picture using the sentence frame: *I see a* _____. See Teacher's Edition p. 106 for scaffolded support with this page.

ELD.PI.K.I.Em, ELD.PI.K.I.Ex, ELD.PI.K.I.Br See the California Standards section

Oral Vocabulary: Food Shapes Guide children to name and talk about the foods in the picture. Ask: *What shapes do you see on the picnic table? What type of food is that?* Ask students to trace the shapes of the items in the picture.

COLLABORATE

Ask partners to draw some favorite foods on a separate piece of paper, and work together to decide what shape or shapes they have. See Teacher's Edition p. 116 for scaffolded support with this page.

1.

2.

3.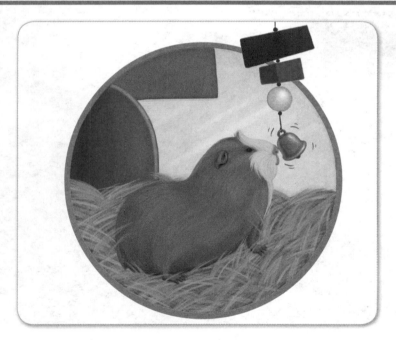

4.

Retell: "We Like Tam" Review the story with children, and work together to retell it. For each picture ask: *What is happening in this picture? What do you think Tam is feeling?*

COLLABORATE

Ask partners to take turns retelling the story. Then invite them to share ways that they would like to play with a pet like Tam. See Teacher's Edition p. 118 for scaffolded support with this page.

ELD.PI.K.6.Em, ELD.PI.K.6.Ex, ELD.PI.K.6.Br; ELD.PI.K.12a.Em, ELD.PI.K.12a.Ex, ELD.PI.K.12a.Br See the California Standards section

_____

- -

_____

Writing Review pages 28-30 in "We Like Tam." Introduce the prompt: *How does Tam feel about Sam?* Ask children to draw a picture of Tam and Sam. Then have them talk about how Tam feels about Sam, and write a label on the line to name that feeling.

Ask partners to describe their drawings and explain how Tam is feeling. Offer this sentence frame: *Tam feels _____ about Sam.* See Teacher's Edition p. 119 for scaffolded support with this page.

ELD.PI.K.6.Em, ELD.PI.K.6.Ex, ELD.PI.K.6.Br; ELD.PI.K.10.Em
See the California Standards section

Keep Moving!

Jump up! Jump down!
Spin all around!
Walk very slowly.
March very fast.

Dance like you
want the song to last.
Jump up! Jump down!
Spin all around!

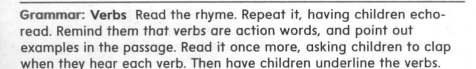

Grammar: Verbs Read the rhyme. Repeat it, having children echo-read. Remind them that verbs are action words, and point out examples in the passage. Read it once more, asking children to clap when they hear each verb. Then have children underline the verbs.

Ask partners to take turns acting out a verb from the rhyme, while the other partner guesses the verb. Children can also think of new action words, and continue the game. See Teacher's Edition p. 125 for scaffolded support with this page.

ELD.PI.K.5.Em, ELD.PI.K.5.Ex, ELD.PI.K.5.Br; ELD.PII.K.3a.Em, ELD.PII.K.3a.Ex, ELD.PII.K.3a.Br See the California Standards section

1.

I like the  .
bus

2.

I like the .
teacher

3.

I like the .
blocks

4.

We like .
school

COLLABORATE

Fluency Track the text as you read the story to children. Then have children echo-read after you, copying your intonation and expression. Ask: *What does the boy like? The boy and the girl?* Ask children to circle the high-frequency word *like*.

Ask one partner to read while the other partner echo-reads, and then switch roles. Then have them use this sentence frame to name something *they* like at school: *I like the _____ .* See Teacher's Edition p. 126 for scaffolded support with this page.

Weekly Concept: World of Bugs

? Essential Question
What kind of bugs do you know about?

Weekly Concept: World of Bugs Guide children to name the bugs in the picture, and describe what they look like. Ask them to name bugs they've seen using this sentence frame: *I saw a* _____ . Then have children draw their own bug into the picture.

Ask partners to share their drawings and describe the bugs they drew. Then have children tell about experiences with other bugs on the page. See Teacher's Edition p. 130 for scaffolded support with this page.

ELD.PI.K.I.Em, ELD.PI.K.I.Ex, ELD.PI.K.I.Br See the California Standards section

Words and Categories: Describing Words Guide children to talk about the features of the bug. Ask: *Where is the shiny part? Which parts are striped? How do you think the different parts would feel to touch?* Have children draw their own imaginary bugs.

Ask partners to talk about the bugs they drew using describing words, such as: *smooth, rough, hard, soft, prickly, red, blue,* etc. See Teacher's Edition p. 133 for scaffolded support with this page.

ELD.PI.K.I.Em, ELD.PI.K.I.Ex, ELD.PI.K.I.Br See the California Standards section

He likes _____ .

Respond to the Text: *I Love Bugs!* Review the story, then have children retell it using the images to guide them. Ask: *What kind of bug is the boy's favorite?* Have children draw their answer in the space provided. Then guide them to complete the sentence.

COLLABORATE

Ask partners to describe their drawings and read their sentences aloud. Then have them take turns retelling the story. See Teacher's Edition p. 136 for scaffolded support with this page.

ELD.PI.K.6.Em, ELD.PI.K.6.Ex; ELD.PI.K.10.Em; ELD.PI.K.12a.Em, ELD.PI.K.12a.Ex, ELD.PI.K.12a.Br See the California Standards section

COLLABORATE

Oral Vocabulary: Bugs that Crawl or Fly Guide children to name and talk about the bugs pictured. Ask: *Which bugs crawl? Which bugs fly? How can you tell the difference?* Have children draw another bug and describe how it moves.

Have partners pretend to be one of the bugs by acting out its movements. Then have them explain how the bug moves. See Teacher's Edition p. 140 for scaffolded support with this page.

ELD.PI.K.I.Em, ELD.PI.K.I.Ex, ELD.PI.K.I.Br See the California Standards section

1.

2.

3.

4.

Retell "Pat" Review the book, then have children use the pictures to retell the story. Remind them to use the pictures in the correct order: *1, 2, 3, 4.* Provide the following sentence frames to guide retelling: *First, Pat _____. Next, Pat _____. Last, Pat _____.*

Ask partners to take turns retelling the story using *first, next,* and *last.* Then have them tell each other their favorite part of the story. See Teacher's Edition p. 142 for scaffolded support with this page.

ELD.PI.K.6.Em, ELD.PI.K.6.Ex; ELD.PI.K.12a.Em, ELD.PI.K.12a.Ex, ELD.PI.K.12a.Br; ELD.PII.K.I.Em See the California Standards section

It has ⎯⎯⎯ a fly ⎯⎯⎯.

ELD.PI.K.6.Em, ELD.PI.K.6.Ex, ELD.PI.K.6.Br; ELD.PI.K.9.Br;
ELD.PI.K.10.Em, ELD.PI.K.10.Ex See the California Standards section

Writing Review "Pat" and then discuss the writing prompt: *Where does Pat live? How do you know? Why do you think Pat lives there?* Say: *Describe Pat's home. What does it have in it?* Have children draw Pat's home and what it has in it, and complete the sentence.

Have partners describe their drawings and read their sentences aloud. Then ask: *Why do you think Pat lives there?* Have partners discuss and then present their ideas to the group. See Teacher's Edition page 143 for scaffolded support with this page.

Busy Bugs

A spider spins.
A grasshopper hops.
A caterpillar wiggles.
They can! Can you?

A bee buzzes.
A cricket chirps.
A butterfly flutters.
Yes, you can, too!

Grammar: Verbs Read the chant aloud. Reread, as children echo-read. Guide children to point out the verbs, and demonstrate the action for each one. Repeat the chant, asking children to clap when they hear a verb. Then have children underline the verbs.

Ask partners to make a list of the actions in the chant. Then have them think of more verbs that describe how insects act. See Teacher's Edition p. 149 for scaffolded support with this page.

ELD.PI.K.5.Em, ELD.PI.K.5.Ex, ELD.PI.K.5.Br; ELD.PII.K.3a.Em
See the California Standards section

50 Unit 2 • Week 3 • Grammar

1.

I see a  .
butterfly

2.

I see a  .
ladybug

3.

I see a 🐝 .
fly

4.

I see Sam!

Fluency Read the passage, modeling the intonation and expression used for exclamations. Remind children to pause at the end of sentences. Then have children read the passage chorally. Ask them to underline the high-frequency word *see*.

ELD.PI.K.5.Em, ELD.PI.K.5.Ex, ELD.PI.K.5.Br; ELD.PIII.K
See the California Standards section

Ask one partner to read while the other partner echo reads, then have them switch roles. Ask: *What do you do at the end of a sentence? How do you change your voice for an exclamation mark?* See Teacher's Edition p. 150 for scaffolded support with this page.

Unit 2 • Week 3 • Fluency **51**

Unit 3

Train Station

Going Places

The Big Idea

What can you learn by going to different places?

Weekly Concept: Rules to Go By

? Essential Question

What rules do we follow in different places?

STOP

COLLABORATE

Weekly Concept: Rules Guide children to talk about the pictures. Ask: *What rules are the people following? How do rules help them stay safe? How are rules helpful at school?* Ask children to circle one person who is following a rule.

Ask partners to point to each child who is following a rule, and name the rule. Then have them tell about a time they followed that rule. See Teacher's Edition p. 158 for scaffolded support with this page.

ELD.PI.K.I.Em, ELD.PI.K.I.Ex, ELD.PI.K.I.Br See the California Standards section

Words and Categories: Things in a School Guide children to name the objects shown. Have them circle objects they would find in a classroom, and explain how to use them. Then have children draw themselves using one or more of the objects.

Ask partners to share their drawings and explain what they're doing in the picture. Offer this sentence frame: *I am using _____ to _____ .* See Teacher's Edition p. 161 for scaffolded support with this page.

COLLABORATE

Respond to the Text: *How Do Dinosaurs Go to School?* Guide children to retell the story. Talk about ways the dinosaurs do and don't cooperate. Ask children to draw a dinosaur who is cooperating, and add a label below it to describe what the dinosaur is doing.

Ask partners to share their drawings and explain how their dinosaur is cooperating. Then have partners tell each other their favorite part of the story. See Teacher's Edition p. 164 for scaffolded support with this page.

ELD.PI.K.6.Em, ELD.PI.K.6.Ex, ELD.PI.K.6.Br; ELD.PI.K.12a.Em, ELD.PI.K.12a.Ex, ELD.PI.K.12a.Br See the California Standards section

1.

2.

3.

4.

COLLABORATE

Oral Vocabulary: Manners Guide children to describe the pictures. Explain that having good manners means following rules and being *polite.* Have children circle the picture that shows bad manners. Then have them draw themselves showing good manners.

Have partners act out the scenes that they drew and explain how they are showing good manners. See Teacher's Edition p. 168 for scaffolded support with this page.

1.

2.

3.

4.

Retell "Can I Pat It?" Guide children to use the pictures to retell the story. Ask: *Can the girl pat a dog? Can she pat a cat? Why can't she pat a fish?* Ask children to circle the animals they could pat.

COLLABORATE

Have partners name other animals, and talk about whether they can or cannot pat them. Offer these sentence frames: *I can pat a _____ . I can't pat a _____ .* See Teacher's Edition p. 170 for scaffolded support with this page.

ELD.PI.K.6.Em, ELD.PI.K.6.Ex, ELD.PI.K.6.Br; ELD.PI.K.12a.Em, ELD.PI.K.12a.Ex, ELD.PI.K.12a.Br See the California Standards section

I can play with it.	I can't play with it.

Writing Review the story "Can I Pat It?" Then, introduce the writing prompt: *Write a new story called "Can I Play with It?" using "Can I Pat It?" as a model.* Have children draw one thing they can play with, and one thing they can't. Guide them to label their pictures.

Have partners share their drawings, and use this sentence frame to ask about each other's work: *Can I play with _____?* Then have them list other objects they can and can't play with. See Teacher's Edition p. 171 for scaffolded support with this page.

ELD.PI.K.2.Em; ELD.PI.K.10.Em, ELD.PI.K.10.Ex; ELD.PII.K.1.Em See the California Standards section

Following Rules

I wait my turn.
I share when I play.
I raise my hand when
I have something to say.

I cross at street corners.
I follow each rule.
I stay safe at home
and school.

Grammar: *Sentences* Read the rhyme, and have children echo-read. Ask children to find the start and end of each sentence. Reread the rhyme, and have children clap when a sentence ends. Then ask children to explain the rules mentioned in the rhyme.

COLLABORATE

Have partners make up a sentence to replace *"I cross at street corners,"* such as *"I wear a helmet"* or *"I pick up my toys."* Then have the pairs share their new sentences with the group. See Teacher's Edition p. 177 for scaffolded support with this page.

ELD.PI.K.2.Em; ELD.PI.K.5.Em, ELD.PI.K.5.Ex, ELD.PI.K.5.Br; ELD.PI.K.9.Em
See the California Standards section

I Like It!

I see it.

I like it!

I like to in it!

run

I like to in it!

jump

Fluency Read the passage with children. Point out the intonation you use for exclamations. Have students read it again, copying your intonation and expression. Ask: *What does the girl like to do?* Have children underline the high-frequency word *to*.

ELD.PI.K.5.Em, ELD.PI.K.5.Ex, ELD.PI.K.5.Br; ELD.PIII.K
See the California Standards section

COLLABORATE

Have partners read the passage to each other until they can read it fluently. Then say: *Pretend that all the exclamation marks are periods. How would you read the story then?* See Teacher's Edition p. 178 for scaffolded support with this page.

? Essential Question

What are the different sounds we hear?

COLLABORATE

Weekly Concept: Sounds Ask children to describe the picture and talk about the sounds in the scene. Have children circle something they would like to hear, and draw an "X" over something that they would not like to hear.

Ask partners to describe sounds they hear as they walk through their neighborhood, and name the things that make the sounds. E.g. *I hear the birds sing; I hear the garbage truck rumble.* See Teacher's Edition p. 182 for scaffolded support with this page.

ELD.PI.K.I.Em, ELD.PI.K.I.Ex, ELD.PI.K.I.Br See the California Standards section

Words and Categories: **Loud and Soft** Guide children to name each object, and discuss whether it makes a loud or soft sound. Then have them draw one thing that makes a loud sound, and one that makes a soft sound.

COLLABORATE

Ask partners to name the objects in their drawings, and imitate the sounds they make. Offer this sentence frame: *The _____ makes a _____ sound.* See Teacher's Edition p. 185 for scaffolded support with this page.

ELD.PI.K.I.Em, ELD.PI.K.I.Ex, ELD.PI.K.I.Br See the California Standards section

Unit 3 • Week 2 • Words and Categories   63

Respond to the Text: *Clang, Clang, Beep, Beep* Review the story.
Ask children to describe the objects, the sounds, and the settings.
Have children draw an object from the book that makes a sound.
Then have them label the object.

Ask partners to take turns retelling the story. Then have them share
their drawings. Ask: *Where might you hear this sound? When might
you hear it?* See Teacher's Edition p. 188 for scaffolded support with
this page.

ELD.PI.K.6.Em, ELD.PI.K.6.Ex,ELD.PI.K.6.Br; ELD.PI.K.10.Em; ELD.PI.K.12a.Em,
ELD.PI.K.12a.Ex, ELD.PI.K.12a.Br See the California Standards section

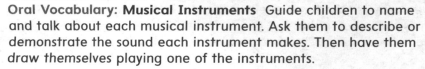

Oral Vocabulary: Musical Instruments Guide children to name and talk about each musical instrument. Ask them to describe or demonstrate the sound each instrument makes. Then have them *draw themselves playing* one of the instruments.

Ask partners to name the musical instrument they would most like to play, and explain their choice. Offer this sentence frame: *I like _____ because _____ .* See Teacher's Edition p. 192 for scaffolded support with this page.

ELD.PI.K.I.Em, ELD.PI.K.I.Ex, ELD.PI.K.I.Br; ELD.PI.K.II.Em
See the California Standards section

1.

2.

3.

4.

COLLABORATE

Retell "Nat and Tip" Review the story, then guide children to use the pictures in sequence to retell it. Ask: *Where do Nat and Tip go? Who do they see first? What sound does the hammer make?* Have them circle something that Nat and Tip like.

Have partners take turns retelling the story. Offer these sentence frames: *Nat and Tip like _____ . Nat and Tip see _____ .* See Teacher's Edition p. 194 for scaffolded support with this page.

ELD.PI.K.6.Em, ELD.PI.K.6.Ex, ELD.PI.K.6.Br; ELD.PI.K.12a.Em, ELD.PI.K.12a.Ex, ELD.PI.K.12a.Br See the California Standards section

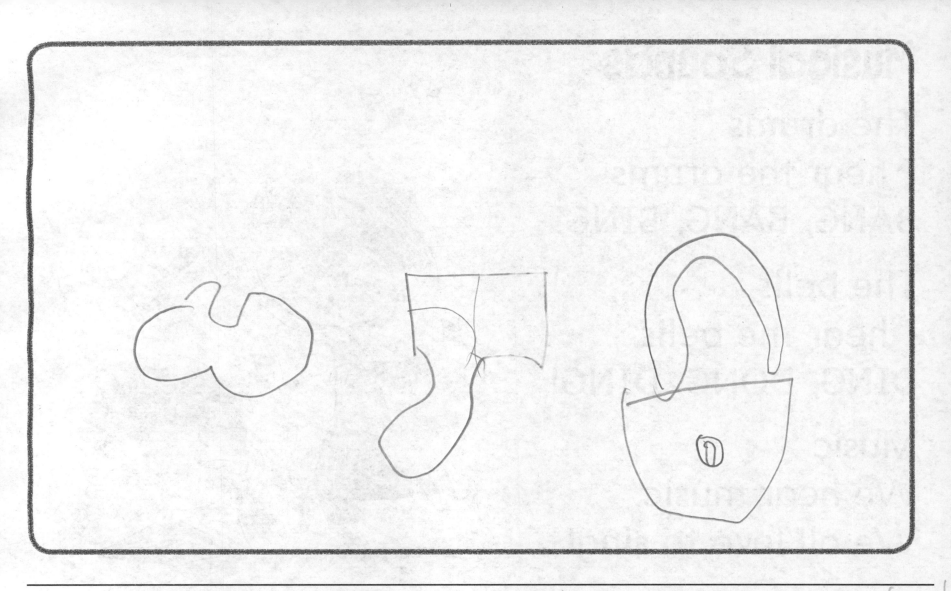

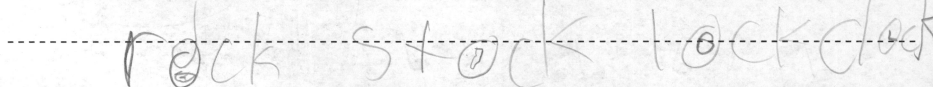

rock stock lock clock

Writing Review pages 29 to 3I of "Nat and Tip." Introduce the prompt: *If you were at the park with Nat and Tip, what sounds would you hear? Use text evidence.* Have children draw two things that make sounds in the story, and use the line to label the drawing.

COLLABORATE

Have partners share their drawings and ideas. Ask: *How do you know what you might hear? What text evidence can you find?* Then ask partners to find other objects in the book that make sounds. See Teacher's Edition p. I95 for scaffolded support with this page.

ELD.PI.K.6.Em, ELD.PI.K.6.Ex, ELD.PI.K.6.Br; ELD.PI.K.I0.Em
See the California Standards section

Musical Sounds

The drums
I hear the drums.
BANG, BANG, BING!

The bells
I hear the bells.
DING, DONG, DING!

Music
We hear music.
We all love to sing!

The Bell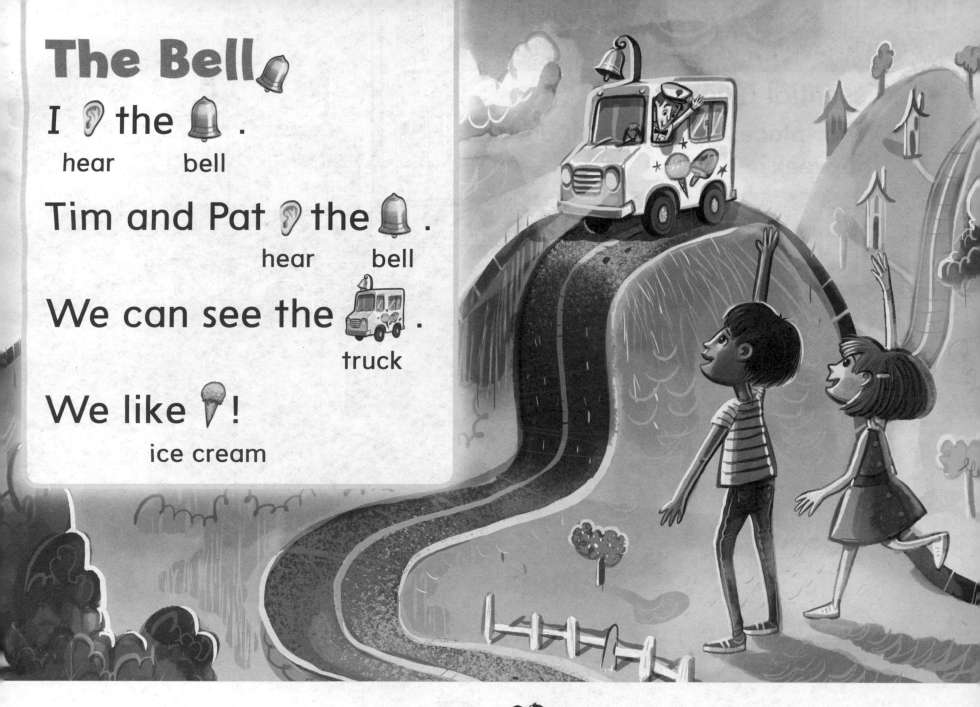

I 👂 the 🔔 .
hear   bell

Tim and Pat 👂 the 🔔 .
hear   bell

We can see the 🚚 .
truck

We like 🍦 !
ice cream

Fluency Read the story. Have children read it again, copying your phrasing and expression. Ask: *How do the children know the truck is coming? What do you think they'll do when the truck reaches them?* Have children circle the high-frequency word *and*.

Have partners take turns reading the story while the other partner echo-reads. Then say: *Talk about what you think will happen next in the story.* See Teacher's Edition p. 202 for scaffolded support with this page.

ELD.PI.K.5.Em, ELD.PI.K.5.Ex, ELD.PI.K.5.Br; ELD.PIII.K
See the California Standards section

Weekly Concept: The Places We Go

? **Essential Question**

What places do you go to during the week?

COLLABORATE

Weekly Concept: Places We Go Guide children to name and talk about the places they see. Ask: *What do you know about this place? Have you been to a place like this?* Have them circle a type of place they like to visit.

Invite partners to tell each other about a place in their town they've visited recently. Encourage them to use details to describe the place, and what they do there. See Teacher's Edition p. 206 for scaffolded support with this page.

ELD.PI.K.I.Em, ELD.PI.K.I.Ex, ELD.PI.K.I.Br See the California Standards section

Restaurant

LIBRARY

Flowers

COLLABORATE

Words and Categories: Neighborhood Places Guide children to talk about the places the dog can go, and the path that leads to the places. Have children choose one place in the neighborhood, and draw a line that leads the dog to that place.

Ask partners to describe the places in the neighborhood, and choose one they would most like to visit. Ask: *Why did you choose that place?* Children can trace the path from the dog to that place. See Teacher's Edition p. 209 for scaffolded support with this page.

ELD.PI.K.I.Em, ELD.PI.K.I.Ex, ELD.PI.K.I.Br; ELD.PI.K.3.Em
See the California Standards section

Respond to the Text: *Please Take Me for a Walk* Review the story, then ask children to retell it using the pictures to guide them. Have children draw another place the dog wanted to go. Then have them write a label on the writing line, naming or describing the place.

72 Unit 3 • Week 3 • Respond to the Text: Big Book

COLLABORATE

Ask partners to describe the place they drew in their picture, and explain why they think the dog would want to go there. See Teacher's Edition p. 212 for scaffolded support with this page.

ELD.PI.K.6.Em, ELD.PI.K.6.Ex, ELD.PI.K.6.Br; ELD.PI.K.10.Em; ELD.PI.K.12a.Em, ELD.PI.K.12a.Ex, ELD.PI.K.12a.Br See the California Standards section

COLLABORATE

Oral Vocabulary: Transportation Guide children to name and describe the different ways of traveling. Ask: *How can people get around their neighborhood? How do you get around your neighborhood?* Have them circle the way they'd most like to travel.

Ask partners to name their favorite ways to travel, and explain why they like these best. Offer the sentence frame: *I like to travel by _____ because _____ .* See Teacher's Edition p. 216 for scaffolded support with this page.

ELD.PI.K.I.Em, ELD.PI.K.I.Ex, ELD.PI.K.I.Br; ELD.PI.K.II.Em
See the California Standards section

1.

2.

3.

4.

COLLABORATE

Retell: "We Go to See Nan" Review the story, then have children use the pictures on this page to retell it. Ask questions such as: *Where was Nan? What did the children see at the bookstore?* Have children circle two clues that tell them where the children are.

Ask partners to retell the story to each other. Have them take turns asking and answering questions such as: *What happened at the beginning/ end of the story?* See Teacher's Edition p. 218 for scaffolded support with this page.

ELD.PI.K.6.Em, ELD.PI.K.6.Ex,ELD.PI.K.6.Br; ELD.PI.K.12a.Em, ELD.PI.K.12a.Ex, ELD.PI.K.12a.Br See the California Standards section

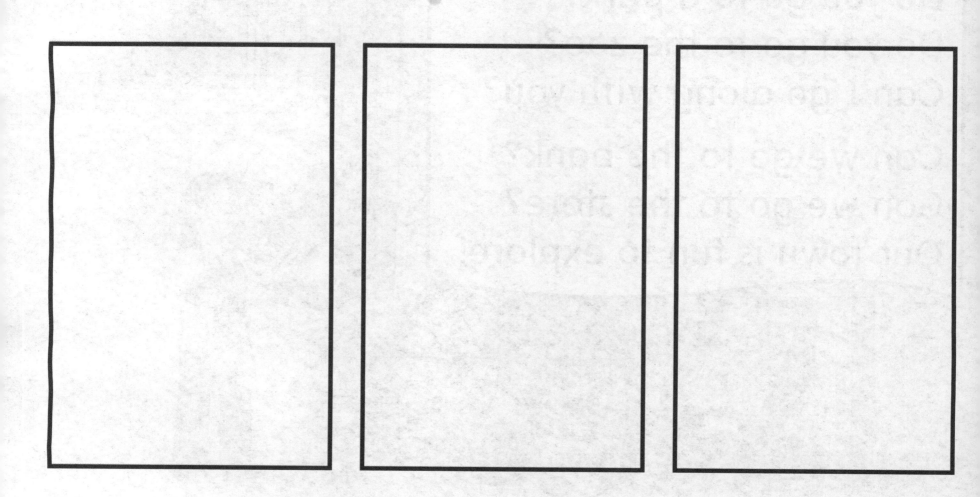

Writing Review "We Go to See Nan." Review the prompt: *Write a journal entry from the girl's point of view. Include evidence from the story.* Guide children to find, draw, and label three pieces of text evidence showing where the girl went, and what she did.

ELD.PI.K.6.Em, ELD.PI.K.6.Ex, ELD.PI.K.6.Br; ELD.PI.K.10.Em, ELD.PI.K.10.Ex See the California Standards section

COLLABORATE

Help partners respond to the prompt orally by describing each of their pictures in order, using these frames: *First/Next/Last I _____.* Ask: *How do you think the girl felt in the story? How do you know?* See Teacher's Edition p. 219 for scaffolded support with this page.

All Through Town

Do you go to a park?
Do you go to the zoo?
Can I go along with you?

Can we go to the bank?
Can we go to the store?
Our town is fun to explore!

Grammar: Sentences Track the text as you read the rhyme. Repeat, as children echo-read. Ask: *What kinds of punctuation marks can end sentences?* Guide children to identify all the sentences in the rhyme. Then have them underline the sentences that are questions.

COLLABORATE

Have partners take turns asking each other where they like to go in their neighborhood, using the sentence frame: *Do you like to go to _____?* Partners should answer in complete sentences. See Teacher's Edition p. 225 for scaffolded support with this page.

ELD.PI.K.3.Em; ELD.PI.K5.Em, ELD.PI.K.5.Ex,ELD.PI.K.5.Br
See the California Standards section

1.

Tim can go in.

2.

Nat and Pat go in.

3.

See the cat!

4.

Can the cat go in?

Fluency Read the story, pointing out the difference in your voice as you read the exclamation and the question. Reread as children echo-read, copying your intonation and expression. Have children circle the high-frequency word *go*.

ELD.PI.K.5.Em, ELD.PI.K.5.Ex, ELD.PI.K.5.Br; ELD.PIII.K
See the California Standards section

Ask partners to take turns reading the story to each other until they can read it fluently. Then have them use their own words to explain the story. Ask: *Where are the mice going? Why can't the cat go in?* See Teacher's Edition p. 226 for scaffolded support with this page.

Around the Neighborhood

The Big Idea

What do you know about the people and places in your neighborhood?

Weekly Concept: Time for Work

? Essential Question

What do people use to do their jobs?

COLLABORATE

Weekly Concept: Time for Work Guide children to talk about the pictures. Ask: *What is each person's job?* Help children name the tools, and describe how the baker or doctor uses each one. Have children circle the tools they have seen in real life.

Guide partners to take turns asking and answering questions. Have one partner point to a tool and use this question frame: *What is a _____ for?* The other partner can use words and gestures to answer. See Teacher's Edition p. 234 for scaffolded support with this page.

ELD.PI.K.I.Em, ELD.PI.K.I.Ex, ELD.PI.K.I.Br See the California Standards section

1.

2.

3.

4.

COLLABORATE

Words and Categories: Vehicles Guide children to name the vehicles pictured, and describe the jobs they do. Talk about other vehicles that are useful tools, such as steamrollers or snowplows. Then, have children draw a vehicle that could help them do a job.

Ask partners to share their drawings, and explain how the vehicles would help them do their jobs. See Teacher's Edition p. 237 for scaffolded support with this page.

ELD.PI.K.I.Em, ELD.PI.K.I.Ex, ELD.PI.K.I.Br See the California Standards section

(tl) PBNJ Productions/Blend Images LLC; (tr) Digital Vision/Getty Images; (bl) Philip Coblentz/age fotostock

COLLABORATE

Respond to the Text: *Whose Shoes? A Shoe for Every Job* Review the book and ask: *Why are different shoes good for different jobs?* Have children draw one of the people from the book, wearing the correct shoes. Then have them write a label naming the person's job.

Ask partners to share their drawings. Say: *Look at the person in your drawing. Why are these shoes good for this person?* Offer this sentence frame: *These shoes are good because* _____ . See Teacher's Edition p. 240 for scaffolded support with this page.

ELD.PI.K.6.Em, ELD.PI.K.6.Ex, ELD.PI.K.6.Br;
ELD.PI.K.10.Em See the California Standards section

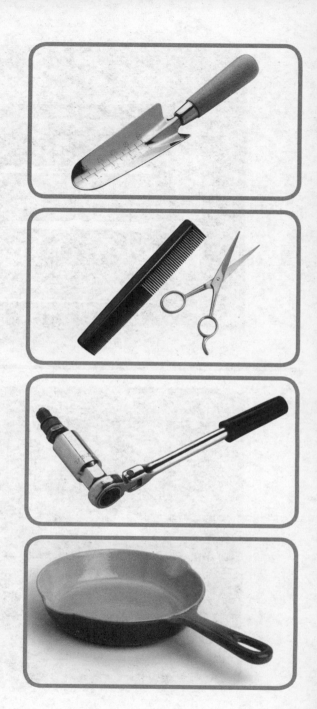

COLLABORATE

Oral Vocabulary: Tools for Jobs Guide children to name each worker and object on the page. Say: *What does this worker do? What tools does he/she need?* Have children draw a line to connect each worker with the right tool for his or her job.

Ask partners to discuss the tools needed for the following jobs: teacher, doctor, and scientist. Offer the sentence frame: *A _____ uses a _____.* See Teacher's Edition p. 244 for scaffolded support with this page.

ELD.PI.K.I.Em, ELD.PI.K.I.Ex, ELD.PI.K.I.Br See the California Standards section

1.

2.

3.

4.

(tl) Stockbyte/Punchstock; (tr) Richard Semik/Alamy; (bl) Richard Hutchings/PhotoEdit Inc.; (br) Code Red/Getty Images

Retell: "Tom on Top!" Guide children to use the pictures to retell the story. Review key words: *firehouse; fire truck; firefighter; hose.* Ask: *What tool helps put water on a fire? What does Tom get on top of?* Have children circle their favorite picture and tell why they like it.

COLLABORATE

Ask partners to point to the photos and use complete sentences to name what they see: *I can see the _____.* Encourage them to identify details in the photos. See Teacher's Edition p. 246 for scaffolded support with this page.

ELD.PI.K.6.Em, ELD.PI.K.6.Ex, ELD.PI.K.6.Br; ELD.PI.K.I2a.Em, ELD.PI.K.I2a.Ex, ELD.PI.K.I2a.Br See the California Standards section

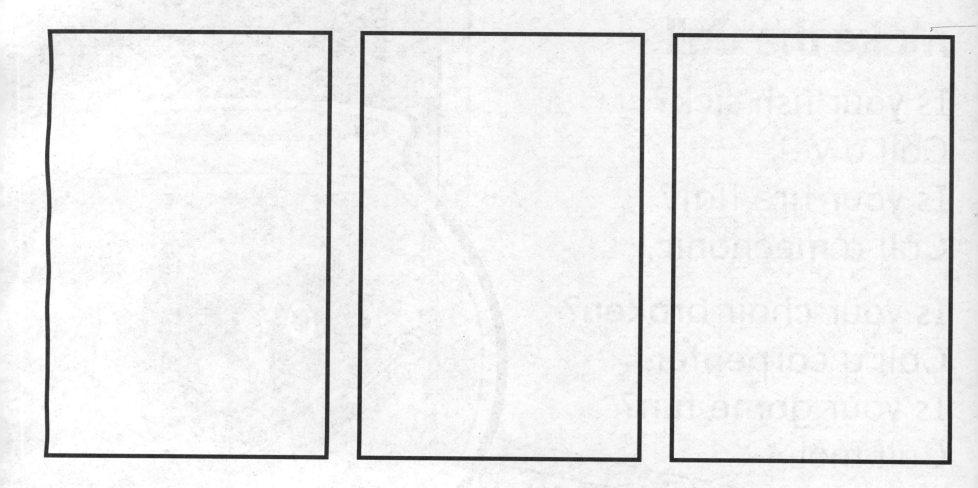

I can see _____.

Writing Review "Tom on Top!" then introduce the prompt: *Write a selection called "The Teacher in Class IA" using "Tom On Top!" as a model.* Help children prepare to write their story by drawing three objects they see in a classroom, then writing about one of them.

ELD.PI.K.I0.Em, ELD.PI.K.I0.Ex; ELD.PII.K.I.Em
See the California Standards section

COLLABORATE

Ask partners to describe their drawings to each other. Have children take turn asking and answering questions using the frames: *What can you see? I can see _____.* See Teacher's Edition p. 247 for scaffolded support with this page.

Unit 4 • Week I • Writing   **85**

Make the Call

Is your fish sick?
Call a vet.
Is your tire flat?
Call a mechanic.

Is your chair broken?
Call a carpenter.
Is your game fun?
Call me!

Grammar: Adjectives Read the selection. Then read it again, as children echo-read. Point out the adjectives that describe nouns: *sick, flat, broken, fun.* Read the selection once more, tracking the words, and ask children to underline each describing word.

Ask partners to use nouns and adjectives to create two new lines for the selection: *Is your [noun] [adjective]? Call a ___ .* Invite each pair to read their lines to the group. See Teacher's Edition p. 253 for scaffolded support with this page.

ELD.PI.K.2.Em; ELD.PI.K.5.Em, ELD.PI.K.5.Ex, ELD.PI.K.5.Br; ELD.PI.K.9.Em; ELD.PII.K.4.Em, ELD.PII.K.4.Ex See the California Standards section

You Can Go on Top

I can go on top.
See the top?
Can you go on top?
You can go on top.
We can go on top!

Fluency Read the selection. Reread it as children echo-read, copying your phrasing and expression. Then have children read it chorally. Ask: *What are the children doing?* Have children circle the high-frequency word *you*.

ELD.PI.K.5.Em, ELD.PI.K.5.Ex, ELD.PI.K.5.Br; ELD.PIII.K
See the California Standards section

COLLABORATE

Ask partners to take turns reading the selection to each other until they can read it fluently. Remind children to pause briefly at the end of each sentence. Then ask them to tell the story in their own words. See Teacher's Edition p. 254 for scaffolded support with this page.

? **Essential Question**

Who are your neighbors?

COLLABORATE

Weekly Concept: Meet Your Neighbors Guide children to talk about the picture. Ask: *Who are the people in this neighborhood?* Encourage children to describe each person. Then have children add to the scene by drawing one of their neighbors.

Have partners take turns asking each other questions about their drawings. For example: *What is your neighbor's name? Where does she/he live? When do you see him/her?* See Teacher's Edition p. 258 for scaffolded support with this page.

ELD.PI.K.I.Em, ELD.PI.K.I.Ex, ELD.PI.K.I.Br See the California Standards section

COLLABORATE

Words & Categories: Fruit Guide children to name and talk about the fruits shown. Ask: *Which fruits do you need to peel or cut? Which have similar colors or shapes? What kind of fruit do you like to eat?* Then have children draw another fruit that they like to eat.

Ask partners to share their drawings and use details to describe them. Encourage their partners to ask questions such as: *Is it crunchy or soft? Does it have seeds? What does it taste like?* See Teacher's Edition p. 26I for scaffolded support with this page.

ELD.PI.K.I.Em, ELD.PI.K.I.Ex, ELD.PI.K.I.Br See the California Standards section

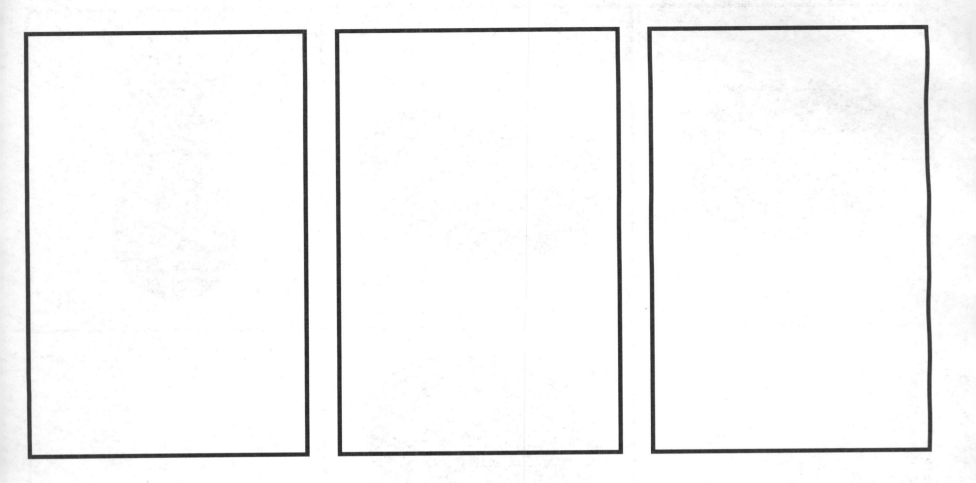

You can _____ .

COLLABORATE

Respond to the Text: *What Can You Do with a Paleta?* Review the story with children. Ask: *What was the setting for the story? Who were the characters?* Guide them to draw three things that you can do with a paleta, then refer to one as they complete the sentence.

Ask partners to use their drawings to retell parts of the story. Encourage them to use details. Ask: *What was your favorite event in the story?* See Teacher's Edition p. 264 for scaffolded support with this page.

ELD.PI.K.6.Em, ELD.PI.K.6.Ex, ELD.PI.K.6.Br; ELD.PI.K.I0.Em; ELD.PI.K.I2a.Em, ELD.PI.K.I2a.Ex, ELD.PI.K.I2a.Br See the California Standards section

90 Unit 4 • Week 2 • Respond to the Text: Big Book

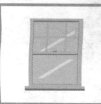       

COLLABORATE

Oral Vocabulary: Parts of a Home Guide children to name and describe the parts of a home shown above. Ask them to find these details in the larger picture. Then encourage students to include details as they draw pictures of their homes.

Ask partners to share their drawings and describe their homes. Students can help each other identify the parts of their homes, using the question frame: *Does your house have a _____ ?* See Teacher's Edition p. 268 for scaffolded support with this page.

1.

2.

3.

4.

Retell "Sid" Review the story with children. Then ask them to use the pictures to retell it. Ask questions such as: *What is Sid's family doing? Who comes to visit? What do Sid and Tod do together?* Ask children to circle one of Sid's new neighbors.

Ask partners to point to the pictures in sequence as they retell the story. Encourage them to use complete sentences. Offer sentence frames such as: *Sid and Mama like _____. Tod can _____.* See Teacher's Edition p. 270 for scaffolded support with this page.

ELD.PI.K.6.Em, ELD.PI.K.6.Ex, ELD.PI.K.6.Br; ELD.PI.K.I2a.Em, ELD.PI.K.I2a.Ex, ELD.PI.K.I2a.Br See the California Standards section

A good neighbor

Writing Review "Sid." Then introduce the prompt: *What are good neighbors like?* Ask: *What does Dan do? What does Dot do? Does Sid like it?* Ask children to draw someone being a good neighbor, then complete the sentence to tell what that person is doing.

ELD.PI.K.2.Em; ELD.PI.K.6.Em, ELD.PI.K.6.Ex, ELD.PI.K.6.Br;
ELD.PI.K.IO.Em, ELD.PI.K.IO.Ex See the California Standards section

COLLABORATE

Ask partners to describe their pictures and read their sentences to each other. Ask: *What else do good neighbors do?* Guide children to draw and write a list. See Teacher's Edition p. 27I for scaffolded support with this page.

My Neighborhood

Can you see
a tiny dog,
a quiet street,
a tall, shady tree,
and a very happy me?

Grammar: *Adjectives* Read "My Neighborhood." Repeat, as children echo-read. Remind children that adjectives describe people, places, or things. Ask: *What adjectives can you find in the selection?* Reread it, tracking the words, and ask children to underline the adjectives.

Ask partners to create a new line for the selection. Have them describe something in their neighborhood using the format: *A [adjective] [noun].* Invite partners to present their lines to the group. See Teacher's Edition p. 277 for scaffolded support with this page.

ELD.PI.K.5.Em, ELD.PI.K.5.Ex, ELD.PI.K.5.Br; ELD.PI.K.9.Em; ELD.PII.K.4.Em, ELD.PII.K.4.Ex See the California Standards section

Pop It, Dot!

Do you see Dot?

Do you see the ?

balloon

Dot can pop it.

Pop! Pop!

See Dot go!

Fluency Read the selection. Model the intonation used for exclamations and questions. Then ask children to read chorally, copying your intonation and expression. Ask: *What did Dot do?* Have children underline the high-frequency word *do*.

ELD.PI.K.5.Em, ELD.PI.K.5.Ex, ELD.PI.K.5.Br;
ELD.PIII.K See the California Standards section

COLLABORATE

Ask partners to take turns reading the story to each other, until they can read it fluently. Ask: *How are you changing your voice when you see an exclamation mark? A question mark?* See Teacher's Edition p. 278 for scaffolded support with this page.

Weekly Concept: Pitch In

? Essential Question

How can people help to make your community better?

LIBRARY

Weekly Concept: Pitch In Guide children to talk about the picture.
Ask: *How are people working together? How are they improving their community?* Have students show how they would help by drawing themselves in the picture.

COLLABORATE

Ask partners to describe their drawings and explain how they are helping. Then children can take turns asking and answering questions about the illustration: *What is he/she doing? She is _____.* See Teacher's Edition p. 282 for scaffolded support with this page.

96 Unit 4 • Week 3 • Weekly Concept

ELD.PI.K.I.Em, ELD.PI.K.I.Ex, ELD.PI.K.I.Br See the California Standards section

Words and Categories: A Construction Site Guide children to name the vehicles. Have them use action words (verbs) to talk about the work being done: *dig, carry, push, lift.* Invite children to circle *the job they would most like to do.*

ELD.PI.K.I.Em, ELD.PI.K.I.Ex, ELD.PI.K.I.Br; ELD.PI.K.II.Em
See the California Standards section

Ask partners to describe the job they circled. Have children explain why they would like it using this frame: *I like this job because _____.* Then they can work together to describe the other jobs shown above. See Teacher's Edition p 285 for scaffolded support with this page.

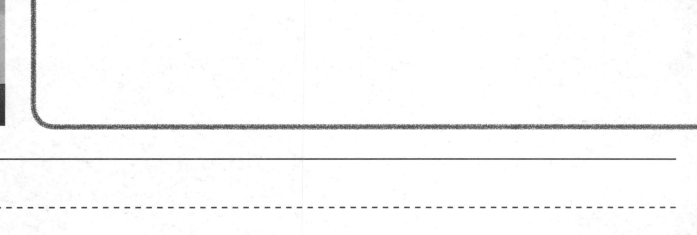

Respond to the Text: *Roadwork* Guide children to use the pictures to retell the story. For each machine, ask: *What kind of work does this do? Answer in a complete sentence: This machine _____.* Have children draw a machine, and describe the work it does on the writing line.

COLLABORATE

Ask partners to share their drawings, and read their descriptions aloud. Ask: *How do the machines in the book work together?* See Teacher's Edition p. 288 for scaffolded support with this page.

ELD.PI.K.6.Em, ELD.PI.K.6.Ex, ELD.PI.K.6.Br;
ELD.PI.K.10.Em See the California Standards section

Oral Vocabulary: Fix it Up Have children compare and contrast the two pictures. Ask: *What is different in the two pictures?* Have students circle the ways that the park has been improved in the *right-hand picture.* Then have them describe the things they circled.

Ask partners to talk about a time they cleaned or fixed something. Guide students to complete the sentence stem: *I helped when I _____ the _____.* See Teacher's Edition p. 292 for scaffolded support with this page.

I.

2.

3.

4.

COLLABORATE

Retell: "I Can, You Can!" Have children retell the story by describing the four pictures in the correct sequence. Ask questions such as: *What do the girl and her mother use to build their sand castle? Who helps them finish the work?*

Ask partners to take turns retelling the story. Encourage them to use complete sentences: *The girl _____ . The girl and her mother _____.* See Teacher's Edition p. 294 for scaffolded support with this page.

ELD.PI.K.6.Em, ELD.PI.K.6.Ex, ELD.PI.K.6.Br; ELD.PI.K.I2a.Em, ELD.PI.K.I2a.Ex, ELD.PI.K.I2a.Br See the California Standards section

The girl _____

_____

. _____

Writing Review "I Can, You Can!" Then, introduce the prompt: *Look at the illustrations. What can you tell about the little girl?* Have children redraw an illustration that shows something about the girl. Then have them complete the sentence with a fact about her.

Ask partners to share their drawings and read their sentences aloud. Then have them work together to find out more about the girl, by finding more clues in the illustrations. See Teacher's Edition p. 295 for scaffolded support with this page..

ELD.PI.K.6.Em, ELD.PI.K.6.Ex, ELD.PI.K.6.Br; ELD.PI.K.IO.Em,
ELD.PI.K.IO.Ex See the California Standards section

Classroom Helper

Tables that are round
A rug that is square
A shelf that is high
A wide, soft chair

Today I will use
a tall, red broom.
I will help to
clean my classroom!

COLLABORATE

Grammar Adjectives Read the rhyme with children. Ask children to find the adjectives that describe objects. Then review them: *round, square, high, wide, soft, tall, red*. Reread the rhyme, tracking the words, and ask children to underline each describing word.

Ask partners to think of other adjectives to describe the tables and rug in the rhyme. Invite them to share their adjectives as you reread the rhyme. See Teacher's Edition p. 301 for scaffolded support with this page.

ELD.PI.K.2.Em; ELD.PI.K.5.Em, ELD.PI.K.5.Ex, ELD.PI.K.5.Br; ELD.PI.K.9.Em; ELD.PII.K.4.Em See the California Standards section

1.

I can not tip the can.

2.

You can not tip it.

3.

We can do it.

4.

The can sip!

plant

COLLABORATE

Fluency Read the selection. Reread as children echo-read, copying your intonation and phrasing. Ask children to tell the story in their own words. Then have them circle the high-frequency words *do* and *you*.

Have partners take turns reading the story to each other until they can read it fluently. Remind children to pause for just a second between sentences. See Teacher's Edition p. 302 for scaffolded support with this page.

ELD.PI.K.5.Em, ELD.PI.K.5.Ex, ELD.PI.K.5.Br; ELD.PIII.K
See the California Standards section

Unit 5

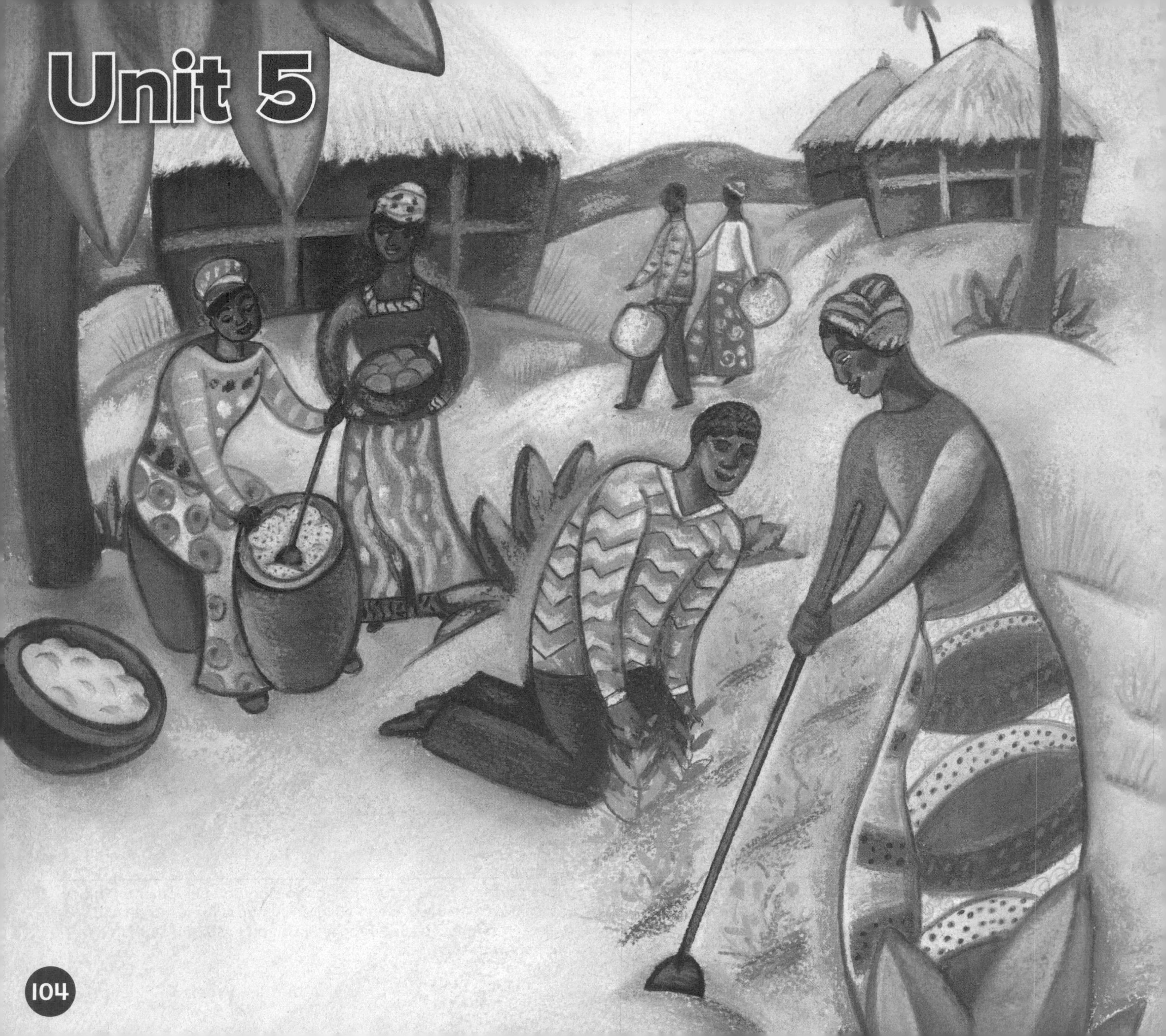

Wonders of Nature

The Big Idea

What kinds of things can you find growing in nature?

Weekly Concept: How Does Your Garden Grow?

? Essential Question

What do living things need to grow?

COLLABORATE

Weekly Concept Guide children to talk about the picture. Say: *See how many different plants you can find. How would you describe these plants? What helps these plants grow?* Ask children to look at the picture and circle three things plants need to grow.

Ask partners to explain how they would care for a potted plant. Ask: *How can you help the plant get what it needs?* Offer the sentence frames: *The plant needs _____. I will _____.* See Teacher's Edition p. 310 for scaffolded support with this page.

ELD.PI.K.I.Em, ELD.PI.K.I.Ex, ELD.PI.K.I.Br See the California Standards section

Words and Categories: Gardening Words Guide children to name and talk about the actions shown in each picture. Ask: *What is the woman doing? How does that help the plant?* Have children draw themselves helping a plant in the last box.

Ask partners to share their drawings and describe what they are doing. Then have them explain how this helps the plant. Offer this sentence frame: *This helps the plant because _____.* See Teacher's Edition p. 313 for scaffolded support with this page.

ELD.PI.K.I.Em, ELD.PI.K.I.Ex, ELD.PI.K.I.Br See the California Standards section

Unit 5 • Week 1 • Words and Categories 107

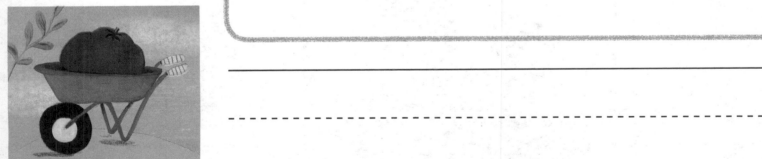

Respond to the Text: *My Garden* Guide children to use the pictures to retell the story. Ask: *What work does the girl do? What does she want to grow?* Have children draw something they would grow in an imaginary garden, and write about it on the writing line.

Ask partners to describe their drawings, starting with this sentence frame: *I grow _____ in my garden.* Children can explain how they would help these gardens grow. See Teacher's Edition p. 316 for scaffolded support with this page.

ELD.PI.K.6.Em, ELD.PI.K.6.Ex, ELD.PI.K.6.Br; ELD.PI.K.IO.Em; ELD.PI.K.I2a.Em, ELD.PI.K.I2a.Ex, ELD.PI.K.I2a.Br See the California Standards section

Oral Vocabulary: **Plant Parts** Guide children to name each plant part: *roots, leaves, flowers, stem, needles, fruit, trunk, buds.* Work together to explain how each part helps the plant. Then have *children* use some of these parts to draw their own plant.

Ask partners to share their drawings and name the parts of their plants. Students can take turns asking and answering questions: *What is this plant part called? This part is called _____ .* See Teacher's Edition p. 320 for scaffolded support with this page.

1.

2.

3.

4.

Retell: "Hop Can Hop!" Have children use the pictures in the correct sequence to retell the story. Ask questions such as: *What does Hop do? Where does Hop go? What do Hop and Dot do at the end of the story?* Have them circle one thing that both Hop and Dot can do.

Ask partners to take turns retelling the story. Encourage children to use complete sentences: *Dot can _____. Hop can _____. Dot and Hop can _____ .* See Teacher's Edition p. 322 for scaffolded support with this page.

ELD.PI.K.6.Em, ELD.PI.K.6.Ex, ELD.PI.K.6.Br; ELD.PI.K.12a.Em, ELD.PI.K.12a.Ex, ELD.PI.K.12a.Br See the California Standards section

I can ____.	My pet can ____.

Writing Review "Hop Can Hop." Introduce the prompt: *Write a story about what you and your make-believe pet can do at the lake.* Have children draw and/or write two things they can do on the left, and two things their pet can do on the right.

Ask partners to share their drawings and describe them using the sentence frames: *I can ____. My pet can ____.* Add a sentence frame for things they and their pet can do: *We can ____.* See Teacher's Edition p. 323 for scaffolded support with this page.

ELD.PI.K.IO.Em, ELD.PI.K.IO.Ex; ELD.PII.K.I.Em
See the California Standards section

The Garden

Carlos works in the garden.
He plants seeds and pulls weeds.

Ava works in the garden.
She gives the flowers a shower.

The sun works in the garden.
It glows and helps plants grow.

Grammar: Pronouns Read the poem aloud. Explain that *Carlos* is a noun, and *he* is a pronoun that stands for Carlos. Have children listen for pronouns as they echo-read each line. Have children circle each pronoun, and underline the noun it replaces.

Ask partners to replace the boy's name with a girl's name, and the girl's name with a boy's name. Then have them change the corresponding pronouns. Partners can read their new lines aloud. See Teacher's Edition p. 329 for scaffolded support with *this* page.

ELD.PI.K.5.Em, ELD.PI.K.5.Ex, ELD.PI.K.5.Br; ELD.PI.K.9.Em
See the California Standards section

I Like My Pot

I like a sip.

I like my pot.

I like the .

sun

I am hot, hot, hot!

Fluency Read the rhyme. Reread, as children echo-read and track the text. Then have children read it chorally. Ask: *What does this rhyme tell you about what plants need?* Have children underline the high-frequency word *my,* and circle words that begin with *h.*

ELD.PI.K.5.Em, ELD.PI.K.5.Ex, ELD.PI.K.5.Br; ELD.PIII.K
See the California Standards section

COLLABORATE

Ask partners to take turns reading the poem to each other until they can read it fluently. Ask: *What does a period tell you to do when you're reading? How about an exclamation mark?* See Teacher's Edition p. 330 for scaffolded support with this page.

Unit 5 • Week 1 • Fluency **113**

? ## Essential Question

How do living things change as they grow?

COLLABORATE

Weekly Concept: Trees Guide children to talk about the pictures. Have them compare the tree and the people in both pictures and describe how each changed.

Ask partners to pretend they're the boy in the pictures. Have them describe what they're doing in each picture. Explain how they, and their tree, changed as they grew. See Teacher's Edition p. 334 for scaffolded support with this page.

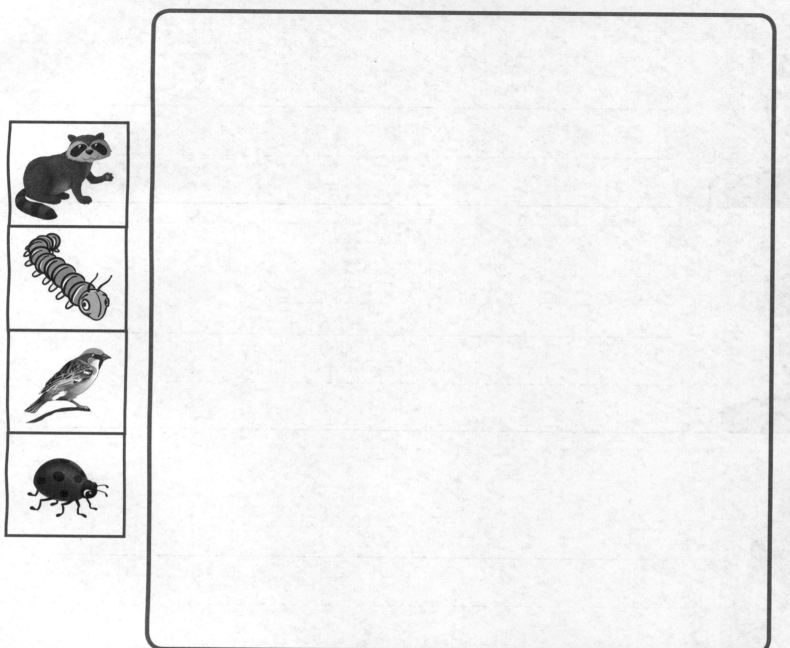

Words and Categories: Animals in Trees Guide children to talk about the animals in the pictures. Say: *You can find all these animals in trees. Does the animal get food from the tree? Shelter? Something else?* Have children draw animals living in a tree.

Ask partners to describe their drawings. Have them take turns asking and answering these questions: *What part of the tree does the animal use? How does the tree help the animal?* See Teacher's Edition p.337 for scaffolded support with this page.

ELD.PI.K.I.Em, ELD.PI.K.I.Ex, ELD.PI.K.I.Br See the California Standards section

1. _____

- -

_____

2. _____

- -

_____

3. _____

- -

_____

Respond to the Text: *A Grand Old Tree!* Review the book. Have children use the images to help them retell it. Ask them to compare and contrast the tree during different parts of the year. Then guide children to write a label describing each tree on this page.

Ask partners to think about a tree they have seen, either in the text or in real life. Have them take turns telling about changes they have observed in the tree over time. See Teacher's Edition p. 340 for scaffolded support with this page.

ELD.PI.K.6.Em, ELD.PI.K.6.Ex, ELD.PI.K.6.Br; ELD.PI.K.12a.Em, ELD.PI.K.12a.Ex, ELD.PI.K.12a.Br; ELD.PII.K.I.Em See the California Standards section

1.

2.

3.

4.

COLLABORATE

Oral Vocabulary: Types of Trees Guide children to talk about the types of trees in the pictures. Have them describe ways they are alike and different. Children can draw a favorite type of tree in the box.

ELD.PI.K.I.Em, ELD.PI.K.I.Ex, ELD.PI.K.I.Br; ELD.PII.K.4.Em
See the California Standards section

Ask partners to share their drawings and describe the trees they drew. Ask: *What adjectives describe your tree?* Provide examples of adjectives that could work: *big, tall, rough, green,* etc. See Teacher's Edition p. 344 for scaffolded support with this page.

1.

2.

3.

4.

(tl) Andy Rouse/The Image Bank/Getty Images; (tr) tbkmedia.de/Alamy; (bl) Annie Katz/Photographer's Choice/Getty Images; (br) Paul Souders/Corbis

COLLABORATE

Retell: "Ed and Ned" Guide children to retell the story, using the pictures in the correct sequence. Model the use of *first*, *next*, and *last* to tell a story. Offer sentence frames: *First, Ed and Ned* _____. *Next, they* _____.

Ask partners to take turns retelling the story. Have them identify their favorite part using this sentence frame: *My favorite part is* _____ *because* _____ . See Teacher's Edition p. 346 for scaffolded support with this page.

ELD.PI.K.6.Em, ELD.PI.K.6.Ex, ELD.PI.K.6.Br; ELD.PI.K.12a.Em, ELD.PI.K.12a.Ex, ELD.PI.K.12a.Br; ELD.PII.K.I.Em See the California Standards section

They have ⸻

⸻

⸻

⸻

⸻

.

Writing Review "Ed and Ned." Introduce the prompt: *Look at Ned and Ed's environment. Do you think they can live somewhere different?* Have children draw Ned and Ed in their environment. Ask them to write about something they have in that environment.

Ask partners to share their work. Have them offer an opinion about the writing prompt, and use evidence to support it: *I think they could/couldn't live somewhere else because _____* . See Teacher's Edition p. 347 for scaffolded support with this page.

ELD.PI.K.10.Em, ELD.PI.K.10.Ex; ELD.PI.K.11.Em, ELD.PI.K.11.Ex, ELD.PI.K.11.Br
See the California Standards section

You and I and the Tree

You and I
can climb
a tree.
We can do it!
You will see!
You and I
and the tree
make three.
We did do it!
Now you see!

Grammar: Pronouns Read the poem. Then reread it, as children echo-read. Remind children that a pronoun takes the place of a noun (a person, place, or thing). Work together to identify the pronouns. Ask children to underline each one.

Ask partners to talk about things they can do together, using these sentence frames: *You and I can _____. We can _____.* *Ask: What pronouns are you using?* See Teacher's Edition p. 353 for scaffolded support with this page.

ELD.PI.K.5.Em, ELD.PI.K.5.Ex, ELD.PI.K.5.Br See the California Standards section

1.

Ned and Ed are in the .

nest

2.

Ned and Ed sit and sit.

3.

Ned and Ed see Mom.

4.

Ned and Ed like it!

COLLABORATE

Fluency Read the selection with children. Have them read it again, copying your intonation and expression. Ask: *What do the baby birds want?* Have children underline the high-frequency word *are* and circle words that have the short *e* sound.

ELD.PI.K.5.Em, ELD.PI.K.5.Ex, ELD.PI.K.5.Br; ELD.PIII.K See the California Standards section

Ask partners to take turns reading the story as the other partner echo-reads. Ask: *Did you pause at the end of each sentence? Did you change your voice when you read the last sentence?* See Teacher's Edition p. 354 for scaffolded support with this page.

Weekly Concept: Fresh from the Farm

? Essential Question

What kinds of things grow on a farm?

COLLABORATE

Weekly Concept: Fresh from the Farm Guide children to talk about the picture. Have them circle and name the different fruits and vegetables they see on the farm. Then guide them to compare and contrast the ways the foods grow.

Ask partners to tell about fruits and vegetables they like to eat. Have them share what they know about how these foods grow. Ask questions like: *Do they grow on trees? Do they grow underground?* See Teacher's Edition p. 358 for scaffolded support with this page.

122 Unit 5 • Week 3 • Weekly Concept

ELD.PI.K.I.Em, ELD.PI.K.I.Ex, ELD.PI.K.I.Br See the California Standards section

Words and Categories: Farm to Market Guide children to describe each picture in sequence. Encourage them to use sequence words such as: *first, next, then, last.* Children can draw a picture showing what happens to the strawberries after they leave the market.

Ask partners to describe their drawings to each other. Then children can take turns describing the sequence of pictures. Model the use of complete sentences and sequence words. See Teacher's Edition p. 361 for scaffolded support with this page.

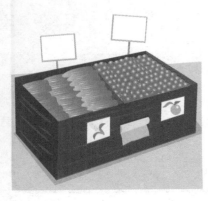

Respond to the Text: *An Orange in January* Guide children to use the pictures to retell the story. Ask: *Where is the orange in the pictures? Where else does the orange go?* Guide children to draw the orange in another place, and label it with the name of the place.

Ask partners to take turns retelling the story. Have them describe their own pictures as part of the retelling. See Teacher's Edition p. 364 for scaffolded support with this page.

ELD.PI.K.6.Em, ELD.PI.K.6.Ex, ELD.PI.K.6.Br; ELD.PI.K.I2a.Em, ELD.PI.K.I2a.Ex, ELD.PI.K.I2a.Br; ELD.PII.K.I.Em See the California Standards section

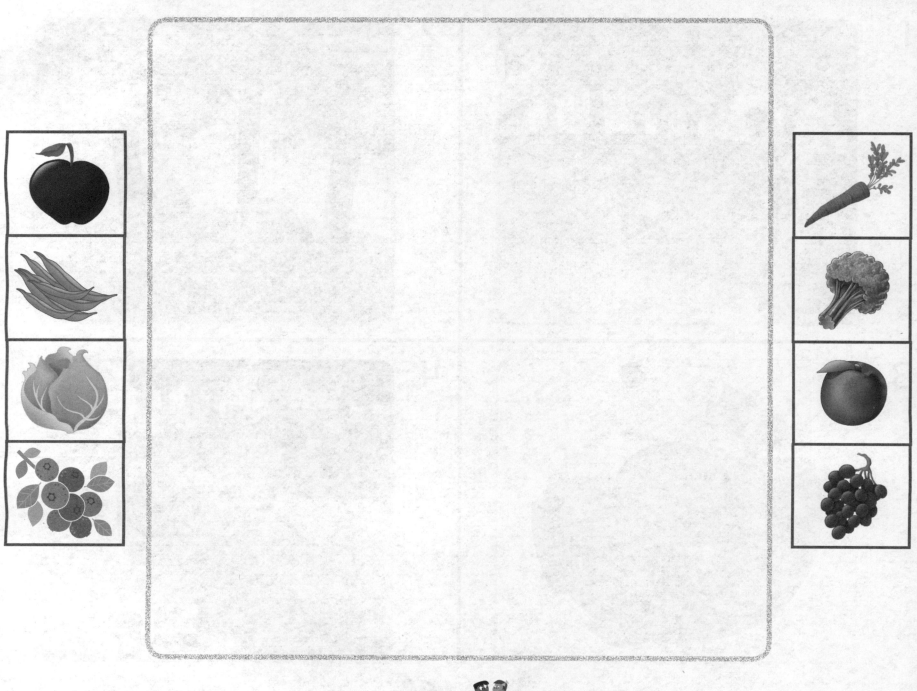

Oral Vocabulary: Fruits and Vegetables Guide children to name and describe the fruits and vegetables shown above. Ask them to circle only the vegetables. Then have children draw themselves *eating* their favorite fruit or vegetable in the space provided.

Ask partners to share their drawings. Encourage them to use details as they describe their favorite fruit or vegetable. See Teacher's Edition p. 368 for scaffolded support with this page.

1.

2.

3.

4.

COLLABORATE

Retell "Ron with Red" Have children use the pictures in the correct sequence to retell the story. Ask questions such as: *Where are Ron and Red? What does Red see? Does Ron see it too?* Have them circle something that Red sees.

Ask partners to take turns retelling the story. Say: *Tell about all the things Ron's Mom and Dad do in the story.* See Teacher's Edition page 370 for scaffolded support with this page.

ELD.PI.K.6.Em, ELD.PI.K.6.Ex, ELD.PI.K.6.Br; ELD.PI.K.12a.Em, ELD.PI.K.12a.Ex, ELD.PI.K.12a.Br See the California Standards section

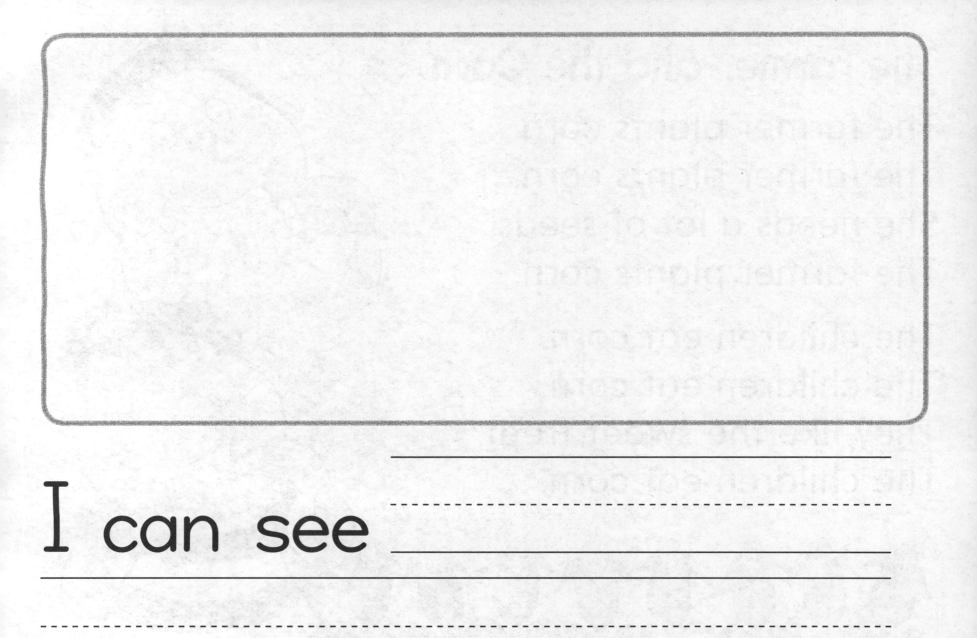

I can see _____

_____

_____

Writing Review "Ron with Red." Then introduce the prompt: *Write a journal entry from Red's point of view about his day at the farm. Use the illustrations and text in the story.* Have children draw Red on the farm, then complete the sentence telling what Red can see.

Ask partners to describe their pictures and read their sentences. Then have them take turns asking and answering these questions: *Where did you go? Who did you go with? What did you do there?* See Teacher's Edition p. 371 for scaffolded support with this page.

ELD.PI.K.IO.Em, ELD.PI.K.IO.Ex; ELD.PII.K.I.Em
See the California Standards section

The Farmer and the Corn

The farmer plants corn.
The farmer plants corn.
She needs a lot of seeds.
The farmer plants corn.

The children eat corn.
The children eat corn.
They like the sweet treat.
The children eat corn.

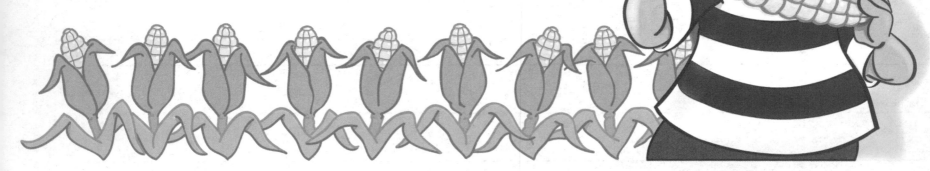

Grammar: *Pronouns* Sing the rhyme to the tune of "The Farmer in the Dell." Sing it again, as children repeat after you. Point out pronouns and the nouns they replace. Sing it again, and pause when you come to a pronoun. Ask: *What noun does this pronoun replace?*

Ask partners to sing the second stanza using one of their names instead of "the children." Have them replace "they" with the appropriate pronoun. (Guide them to change the verbs as needed.) See Teacher's Edition p. 377 for scaffolded support with this page.

128 Unit 5 • Week 3 • Grammar

ELD.PI.K.5.Em, ELD.PI.K.5.Ex, ELD.PI.K.5.Br See the California Standards section

My Fat Pet

Can you see my pet Nat?
He is red and fat.
Nat can sit with Pop.
He can not sit on top!

COLLABORATE

Fluency Read the selection, modeling the correct intonation for questions and exclamations. Have children read it, copying your intonation and expression. Have them underline the high-frequency words *he* and *with* and circle words beginning with *f* or *r*.

Ask partners to take turns reading the story until they can read it fluently. Ask them to show how they change their voices when they see question marks and exclamation marks. See Teacher's Edition p. 378 for scaffolded support with this page.

ELD.PI.K.5.Em, ELD.PI.K.5.Ex, ELD.PI.K.5.Br;
ELD.PIII.K See the California Standards section

Weather for all Seasons

The Big Idea

How do weather and seasons affect us?

? Essential Question

How are the seasons different?

COLLABORATE

Weekly Concept: The Four Seasons Guide children to compare and contrast the four pictures. Ask: *How does the tree change? Why do you think it changes?* Review the four seasons. Then ask students to name the season shown in each image, and circle their favorite.

Ask partners to describe their favorite season. Have them explain why they like it. Offer the sentence frame: *I like _____ because _____.* See Teacher's Edition p. 386 for scaffolded support with this page.

1.

cold   cool   hot   warm

2.

cold   cool   hot   warm

COLLABORATE

Words and Categories: **Temperature Words** Point to each picture and read its label. Ask students to describe each object, using temperature words: E.g. *It's a glass of cool water.* Then have them draw objects that are cold, cool, hot, and warm in the empty boxes.

Ask partners to share their drawings, and use temperature words to describe them. Partners can take turns asking and answering questions about the drawings: *What temperature is this? It is _____.* See Teacher's Edition p. 389 for scaffolded support with this page.

They _____

_____ .

Respond to the Text *Mama, Is It Summer Yet?* Guide children to use the pictures to retell the story. Ask: *How can you tell which season it is?* Then ask: *What do the mother and son do in summer?* Have children draw and write their answer to this question.

Ask partners to describe their drawings and read their sentences aloud. Then say: *Tell about what* you *like to do in the summer.* See Teacher's Edition p. 392 for scaffolded support with this page.

134 Unit 6 • Week I • Respond to the Text: Big Book

ELD.PI.K.6.Em, ELD.PI.K.6.Ex, ELD.PI.K.6.Br; ELD.PI.K.I2a.Em, ELD.PI.K.I2a.Ex, ELD.PI.K.I2a.Br See the California Standards section

January February March April

May June July August

September October November December

Oral Vocabulary: Months of the Year Track the images and read the names of the months, as children echo-read. Talk about each image. Ask: *What does this picture tell you about the month? What season is this month in?*. Have children circle their birthday month.

Ask partners to take turns reading the names of the months. Then have each student pick one month that they like, and explain why they like it. Offer this frame: *I like _____ because _____*. See Teacher's Edition p. 396 for scaffolded support with this page.

ELD.PI.K.I.Em, ELD.PI.K.I.Ex, ELD.PI.K.I.Br; ELD.PI.K.II.Em See the California Standards section

1.

2.

3.

4.

(tl) Ed Bock/Corbis; (tr) Colleen Cahill/Design Pics/Getty Images; (bl) Fancy/Age Fotostock; Doable/amanaimages/Getty Images; (br) Doable/amanaimages/Getty Images

Retell "Is It Hot?" Have children use the pictures to retell the selection. Ask questions such as: *How can you tell if it is hot or cool outside? How does hot weather change what people do?*

COLLABORATE

Ask partners to take turns retelling the story. Then have each student choose one image, and tell about a time they did something like that. See Teacher's Edition p. 398 for scaffolded support with this page.

ELD.PI.K.6.Em, ELD.PI.K.6.Ex, ELD.PI.K.6.Br; ELD.PI.K.12a.Em, ELD.PI.K.12a.Ex, ELD.PI.K.12a.Br See the California Standards section

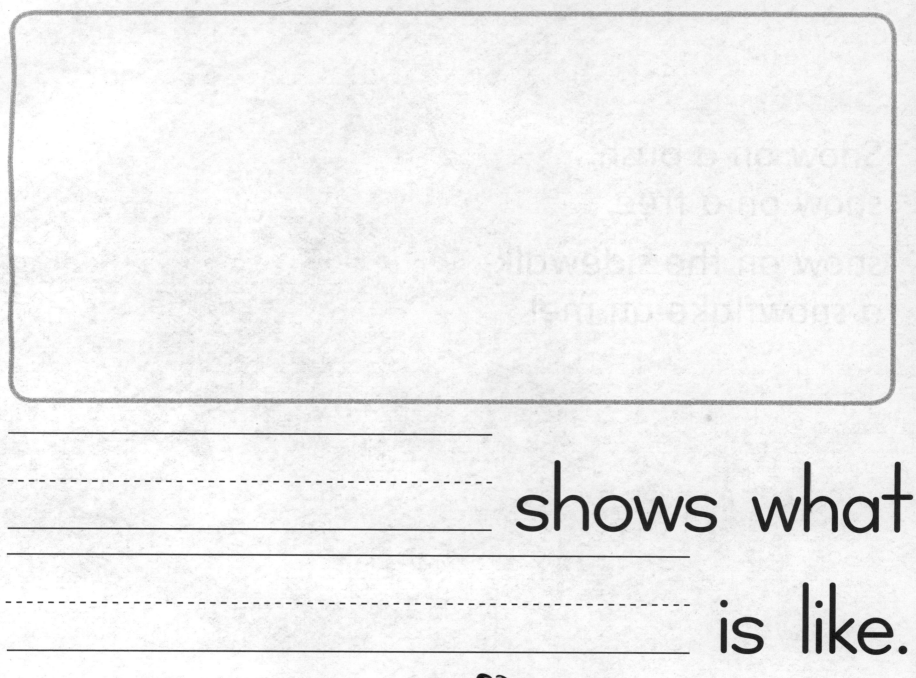

shows what

is like.

Snow

Snow on a bush,
snow on a tree,

snow on the sidewalk,
a snowflake on me!

COLLABORATE

Grammar: Nouns Read the selection. Ask children to name the season shown. Reread the selection as children echo-read. Help children identify the naming words (nouns). Then reread once more, tracking the words, and ask children to underline each noun.

Ask partners to write a poem about rain that uses nouns. Guide them to use "Snow" as a model. Have partners present their poems to the group, and point out the nouns. See Teacher's Edition p. 405 for scaffolded support with this page..

ELD.PI.K.2.Em, ELD.PI.K.2.Ex; ELD.PI.K.5.Em, ELD.PI.K.5.Ex; ELD.PI.K.9.Em, ELD.PI.K.9.Ex; ELD.PII.K.4.Em See the California Standards section

1.

I like my little cat.

2.

He can sit on my lap.

3.

He can nap in bed.

4.

My little cat is hot!

COLLABORATE

Fluency Read the story with children. Reread as children echo-read, copying your intonation and expression. Ask: *How does the boy feel about his cat? Why is the cat hot?* Have children underline the high-frequency words *is* and *little.*

Have partners take turns reading the story to each other until they can read it fluently. Then ask them to read it together, in unison. See Teacher's Edition p. 406 for scaffolded support with this page.

ELD.PI.K.5.Em, ELD.PI.K.5.Ex, ELD.PI.K.5.Br; ELD.PIII.K See the California Standards section

Weekly Concept: What's the Weather?

? Essential Question

What happens in different kinds of weather?

COLLABORATE

Weekly Concept Guide children to compare and contrast the pictures. Ask: *What is the same about the pictures? Different? Which shows windy weather? How can you tell?* Have children circle clues in each picture that tell them what the weather is like.

Ask partners to share the clues they circled. Ask: *What does each clue tell you?* Then invite children to talk about what happens in other kinds of weather, such as snow or hot sun. See Teacher's Edition p. 410 for scaffolded support with this page.

ELD.PI.K.I.Em, ELD.PI.K.I.Ex, ELD.PI.K.I.Br See the California Standards section

Words and Categories: The Senses Guide children to talk about the picture. Ask: *What do the boy and his father hear/ smell/ taste/ feel/ see?* Ask children to choose one sense and circle objects they could experience with that sense.

COLLABORATE

Ask partners to draw the same scene on a sunny day. Ask: *What could the boy and his father hear/ smell/ taste/ feel/ see in your picture?* See Teacher's Edition p. 413 for scaffolded support with this page.

ELD.PI.K.I.Em, ELD.PI.K.I.Ex, ELD.PI.K.I.Br See the California Standards section

Respond to the Text *Rain* Review the book. Then have children use the pictures to retell it. Ask: *What does each animal do after the rain?* Have children draw a picture of one animal after the rain. Then ask them to write a sentence telling what their animal does.

Ask partners to describe their drawings and read their sentences aloud. Invite children to act out what their animal does after the rain. See Teacher's Edition p. 416 for scaffolded support with this page.

ELD.PI.K.6.Em, ELD.PI.K.6.Ex, ELD.PI.K.6.Br; ELD.PI.K.12a.Em, ELD.PI.K.12a.Ex, ELD.PI.K.12a.Br See the California Standards section

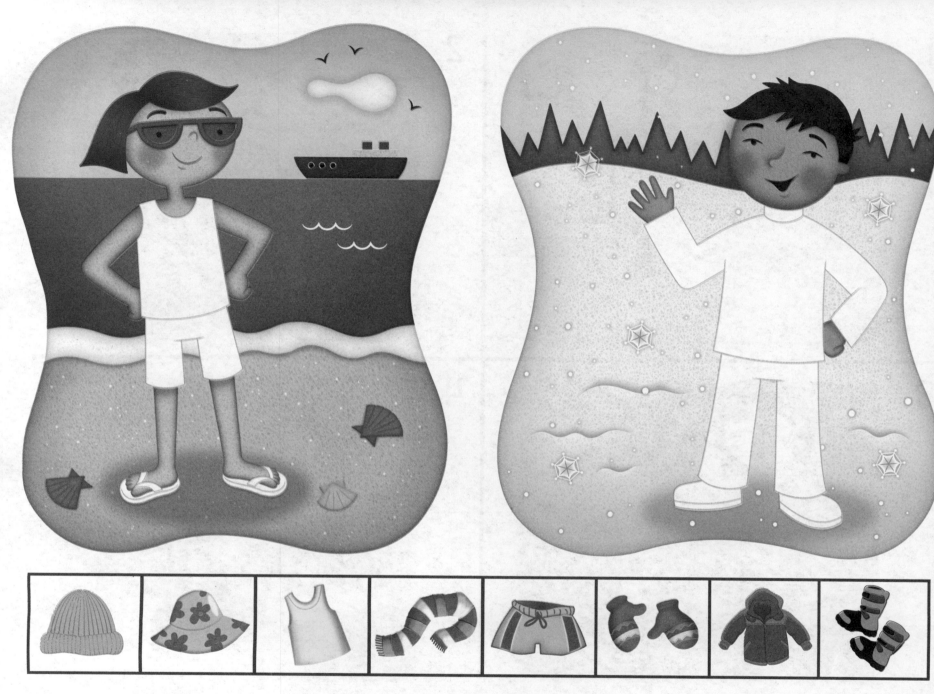

Oral Vocabulary: **Clothing** Help children to name the types of clothing. Ask: *Which of these clothes would be worn on a warm, sunny day? Which would be worn on a cold, snowy day?* Have children draw the appropriate clothing on the two figures.

COLLABORATE

Ask partners to share their drawings. Ask: *What kinds of clothes do you wear in cold weather? Warm weather? Wet weather?* See Teacher's Edition p. 420 for scaffolded support with this page.

ELD.PI.K.I.Em, ELD.PI.K.I.Ex, ELD.PI.K.I.Br See the California Standards section

1.

2.

3.

4.

Retell: "Kim and Nan" Have children use the pictures in the correct sequence to retell the story. Ask questions such as: *What did Kim have? Where did Kim and Nan go? What did they do?*

COLLABORATE

Ask partners to take turns retelling the story, using complete sentences. Offer sentence starters from the story: *Kim has _____ . Kim sat _____ . Kim ran _____ .* See Teacher's Edition p. 422 for scaffolded support with this page.

ELD.PI.K.6.Em, ELD.PI.K.6.Ex, ELD.PI.K.6.Br; ELD.PI.K.I2a.Em, ELD.PI.K.I2a.Ex, ELD.PI.K.I2a.Br See the California Standards section

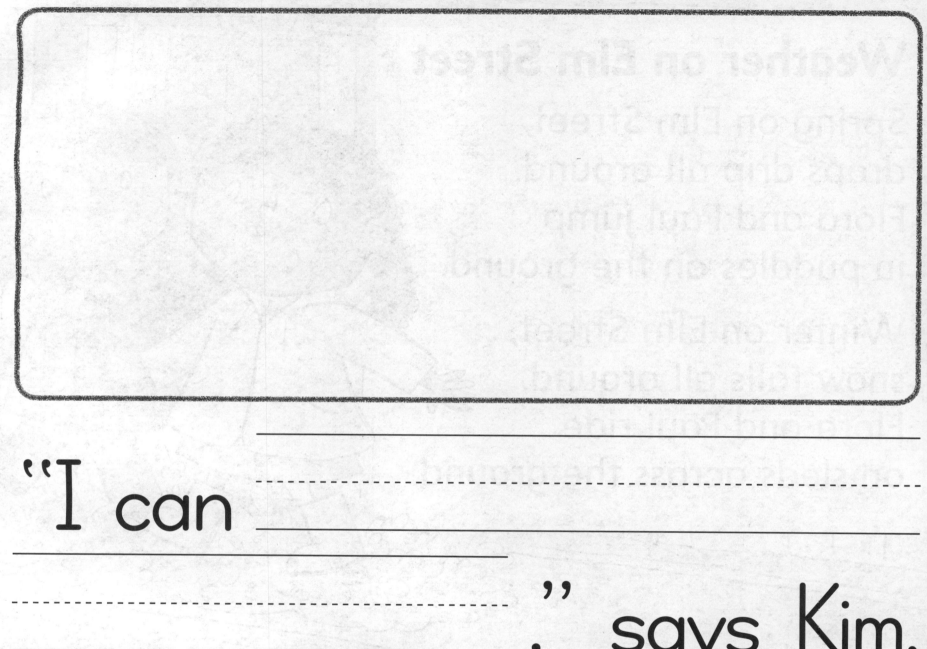

"I can _____

_____ ," says Kim.

Writing Review the story. Introduce the prompt: *Tell what Kim and Nan might say to each other about their next adventure. Use dialogue.* Guide children to draw Kim and Nan having a new adventure, and complete the sentence.

ELD.PI.K.IO.Em, ELD.PI.K.IO.Ex; ELD.PII.K.I.Em
See the California Standards section

Ask partners to pretend they are Kim and Nan, on a new adventure. Have them respond to the prompt orally using sentences such as: *I can _____ . I have _____ . I ran _____ .* See Teacher's Edition p. 423 for scaffolded support with this page.

Weather on Elm Street

Spring on Elm Street,
drops drip all around.
Flora and Paul jump
in puddles on the ground.

Winter on Elm Street,
snow falls all around.
Flora and Paul ride
on sleds across the ground.

COLLABORATE

Grammar: Proper Nouns Read the rhyme. Reread, as children echo-read. Point out the proper nouns: *Elm Street, Flora, Paul.* Reread the rhyme, tracking the words. Ask children to underline each proper noun, and circle the remaining nouns.

Ask partners to create a sentence describing the weather today, using your school's street name (a proper noun). Use the first sentence of the rhyme as a model. See Teacher's Edition p. 429 for scaffolded support with this page.

ELD.PI.K.2.Em, ELD.PI.K.2.Ex; ELD.PI.K.5.Em, ELD.PI.K.5.Ex, ELD.PI.K.5.Br; ELD.PII.K.4.Em See the California Standards section

She Can Do It!

Rick was a little sad.
Can Kit get it?
Kit can see it.
She can pick it up.
Rick is not sad!

Fluency Read the selection. Model the differences among reading a question, an exclamation, and a statement. Reread as children echo-read, copying your expression. Ask: *Why was Rick sad?* Have children underline the high-frequency words *she* and *was*.

Ask partners to take turns reading the selection to each other until they can read it fluently. Ask them to tell what happened, in their own words. See Teacher's Edition p. 430 for scaffolded support with this page.

ELD.PI.K.5.Em, ELD.PI.K.5.Ex, ELD.PI.K.5.Br;
ELD.PIII.K See the California Standards section

Weekly Concept: Stormy Weather

? Essential Question

How can you stay safe in bad weather?

Weekly Concept: Stormy Weather Guide children to talk about the picture. Ask: *What is the weather like? What are the mom and girl doing? How are they staying safe?* Have children circle a clue that tells them it's cold outside.

148 Unit 6 • Week 3 • Weekly Concept

COLLABORATE

Have partners tell what they do in different kinds of bad weather. E.g.: *When it rains, I _____. When there is lightning, I _____. During a snowstorm, I _____.* See Teacher's Edition p. 434 for scaffolded support with this page.

1.

2.

3.

4.

Words and Categories: Clouds Use adjectives (describing words) to describe each cloud shown. Ask: *What types of weather do these clouds bring?* Have children draw a type of cloud that they've seen.

Invite partners to share their drawings. Provide adjectives to help children describe the clouds (e.g. *fluffy, dark, white, thick, flat, big*). See Teacher's Edition p. 437 for scaffolded support with this page.

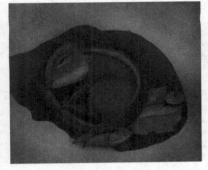

It _____

- -

_____ .

COLLABORATE

Respond to the Text: *Waiting Out the Storm* Ask children to point to the pictures as they retell the story. Ask: *How do animals protect themselves?* Have children draw one animal protecting itself. Then have them complete the sentence to tell what the animal does.

Ask partners to describe their drawings and read their sentences aloud. Guide partners to compare and contrast the ways their two animals protect themselves. See Teacher's Edition p. 440 for scaffolded support with this page.

ELD.PI.K.6.Em, ELD.PI.K.6.Ex, ELD.PI.K.6.Br; ELD.PI.K.10.Em, ELD.PI.K.10.Ex See the California Standards section

COLLABORATE

Oral Vocabulary: Storms Guide children to describe the photos, naming the different kinds of bad weather. Talk about the effects of different kinds of storms. Ask: *How could you stay safe during these storms?* Have children draw a type of storm that they've seen.

Invite partners to describe their drawings, and tell about what they did during the storm. See Teacher's Edition p. 444 for scaffolded support with this page.

ELD.PI.K.I.Em, ELD.PI.K.I.Ex, ELD.PI.K.I.Br See the California Standards section

1.

2.

3.

4.

COLLABORATE

Retell: "Mack and Ben" Have children use the pictures in the correct sequence to retell the story. Ask questions such as: *Why can't Mack and Ben play outside? What do they do inside the house? How does the story end?*

Have partners take turns retelling the story. Offer this sentence frame: *The weather was _____ , so Mack and Ben _____.* See Teacher's Edition p. 446 for scaffolded support with this page.

ELD.PI.K.6.Em, ELD.PI.K.6.Ex, ELD.PI.K.6.Br; ELD.PI.K.12a.Em, ELD.PI.K.12a.Ex, ELD.PI.K.12a.Br See the California Standards section

Ben says, "We can _____

_____

_____ ,"

_____ .

Writing Review "Mack and Ben." Then, introduce the prompt: *What might Ben and Mack say about what they can do now that the weather has cleared up?* Guide children to draw one thing Ben and Mack can do, and write what Ben says about it.

ELD.PI.K.2.Em, ELD.PI.K.2.Ex; ELD.PI.K.IO.Em, ELD.PI.K.IO.Ex
See the California Standards section

COLLABORATE

Ask partners to share their work. Then ask: *What else could Ben and Mack do in nice weather?* Have partners use dialogue to describe their ideas: *Ben says, "_____." Mack says, "_____."* See Teacher's Edition p. 447 for scaffolded support with this page.

Unit 6 • Week 3 • Writing   153

The Storm

Strong winds may blow.
Rain may flow.
Branches may break.
And windows may shake.

Lightning may flash
in the sky.
But I'll be inside,
safe and dry!

COLLABORATE

Grammar: Plural Nouns Read the rhyme. Repeat it as children echo-read. Ask: *What is happening in this rhyme?* Then ask children to find the plural nouns: *winds, branches, windows.* Reread, tracking the words together, and ask them to underline plural nouns.

Have partners list plural nouns that could describe a storm (e.g. *raindrops, snowflakes, puddles*). Then have them use one noun in a sentence. Children can present their sentences to the group. See Teacher's Edition p. 453 for scaffolded support with this page.

ELD.PI.K.2.Em, ELD.PI.K.2.Ex; ELD.PI.K.5.Em, ELD.PI.K.5.Ex, ELD.PI.K.5.Br; ELD.PI.K.9.Em; ELD.PII.K.4.Em See the California Standards section

She Kicks!

Little Pam is with us.
Pam can run.
Go Pam, go!
She can kick.
Kick it, Pam!

COLLABORATE

Fluency Track the text as you read the story. Ask children to point out the exclamation marks. Reread as children echo-read, copying your intonation and expression. Have them circle the high-frequency words *is, little,* and *she.*

Ask partners to take turns reading the story until they can read it fluently. Ask: *How do you change your voice when you see an exclamation mark?* See Teacher's Edition p. 454 for scaffolded support with this page.

ELD.PI.K.5.Em, ELD.PI.K.5.Ex, ELD.PI.K.5.Br;
ELD.PIII.K See the California Standards section

Unit 7

The Animal Kingdom

The Big Idea

What are different kinds of animals?

? Essential Question

How are some animals alike and how are they different?

Weekly Concept: Baby Animals Guide children to name, and talk about, the animals in the picture. Ask: *How are the baby animals like the adults? How are the adult animals alike? How are they different?* Have children circle the two adults they think are most alike.

Ask children to name their favorite animal on the page and describe it to their partners. Encourage children to explain what they like about the animal: *I like the _____ because _____.* See Teacher's Edition p. 462 for scaffolded support with this page.

ELD.PI.K.I.Em, ELD.PI.K.I.Ex, ELD.PI.K.I.Br; ELD.PI.K.II.Em
See the California Standards section

red fox   **cat**   **tiger**   **gorilla**

kangaroo   **chipmunk**   **seal**   **dolphin**

COLLABORATE

Words and Categories: Kinds of Mammals Read the animal names. Explain that these animals belong to a category called *mammals*. Ask children to compare and contrast the mammals: *How are they alike? Different?* Have them circle animals that use legs to move.

Ask partners to choose two animals to compare and contrast. Have them list ways the animals are alike and different. See Teacher's Edition p. 465 for scaffolded support with this page.

ELD.PI.K.I.Em, ELD.PI.K.I.Ex, ELD.PI.K.I.Br See the California Standards section

COLLABORATE

Respond to the Text: *ZooBorns!* Guide children to describe each of the animals in the photos. Ask: *What is special about this type of animal?* Have children draw an animal from the book and label one special feature.

Ask partners to describe their drawings, and explain what's special about their animals. See Teacher's Edition p. 468 for scaffolded support with this page.

ELD.PI.K.6.Em, ELD.PI.K.6.Ex, ELD.PI.K.6.Br; ELD.PI.K.10.Em
See the California Standards section

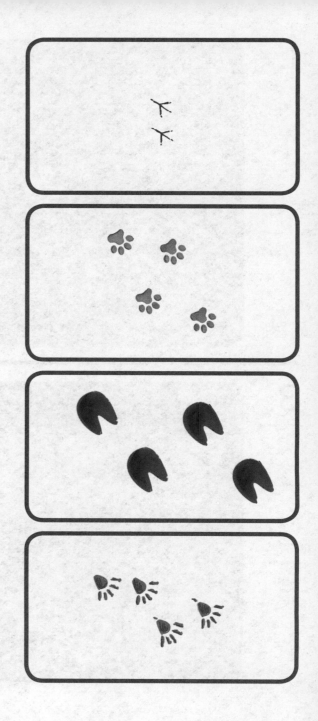

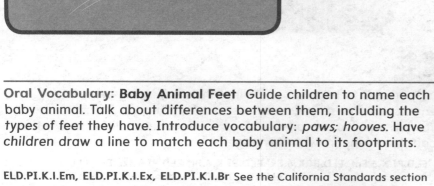

Oral Vocabulary: Baby Animal Feet Guide children to name each baby animal. Talk about differences between them, including the types of feet they have. Introduce vocabulary: *paws; hooves.* Have *children* draw a line to match each baby animal to its footprints.

COLLABORATE

Ask partners to take turns naming an animal and describing its feet. See Teacher's Edition p. 472 for scaffolded support with this page.

1.

2.

3.

4.

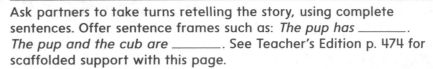

Retell "A Pup and a Cub" Have children use the pictures in the correct sequence to retell the selection. Ask questions, such as: *What is the cub doing? What are the cub and pup doing?*

Ask partners to take turns retelling the story, using complete sentences. Offer sentence frames such as: *The pup has _____. The pup and the cub are _____.* See Teacher's Edition p. 474 for scaffolded support with this page.

ELD.PI.K.6.Em, ELD.PI.K.6.Ex, ELD.PI.K.6.Br; ELD.PI.K.12a.Em, ELD.PI.K.12a.Ex, ELD.PI.K.12a.Br See the California Standards section

Same

Different

is the same.

Writing Review "A Pup and a Cub." Then, introduce the prompt: *How are the wolf pup and the lion cub the same, and different?* Have children draw one thing that's the same, and one thing that's different. Then have them complete the sentence.

Ask partners to share their drawing and writing. Offer these sentence frames: *The pup and the cub are the same because* _____. *They are different because* _____. See Teacher's Edition p. 475 for scaffolded support with this page.

ELD.PI.K.6.Em, ELD.PI.K.6.Ex; ELD.PI.K.IO.Em, ELD.PI.K.IO.Ex See the California Standards section

My Chick

Inside the egg,
my chick is ready.
It pecks and pecks,
strong and steady.

The shell cracks.
My chick comes out.
It will see what the
world is all about.

Grammar: Verbs Track the words as you read the rhyme. Repeat, as children echo-read. Then guide children to find the verbs. Point out that when only one chick is acting, the verb ends in –s. Have children underline all the verbs in the rhyme.

COLLABORATE

Ask partners to suggest a new action word to replace a verb in one of the lines. Reread the rhyme. Ask each pair to share its new line with the group. See Teacher's Edition p. 481 for scaffolded support with this page.

ELD.PI.K.5.Em, ELD.PI.K.5.Ex, ELD.PI.K.5.Br; ELD.PI.K.9.Em;
ELD.PII.K.3a.Em See the California Standards section

My Pup

My pup is little.
He is fun, fun, fun.
He can go in mud.
He can run, run, run.

I have a lap for my pup.
And you can see.
The mud, mud, mud
can go on me!

COLLABORATE

Fluency Read the story. Reread as children echo-read, copying your phrasing. Point out how you pause after commas and periods. Have children underline the high-frequency words *have* and *for,* then *circle* words with the short *u* sound.

Ask partners to take turns reading the story until they can read it fluently. Ask: *What is happening in the selection? How do you think the boy feels?* See Teacher's Edition p. 482 for scaffolded support with this page.

ELD.PI.K.5.Em, ELD.PI.K.5.Ex, ELD.PI.K.5.Br; ELD.PIII.K See the California Standards section

Weekly Concept: Pet Pals

? Essential Question

How do you take care of different kinds of pets?

COLLABORATE

Weekly Concept: Pet Pals Guide children to talk about the picture. Ask: *How is this family taking care of its pets?* For each pet ask: *What kind of pet is this? What does this pet need?* Children can circle the pet they would like to have.

Ask partners to talk about pets they have, or would like to have. Ask: *How will you care for your pet?* Offer sentence frames: *My pet needs _____. I will _____.* See Teacher's Edition p. 486 for scaffolded support with this page.

ELD.PI.K.I.Em, ELD.PI.K.I.Ex, ELD.PI.K.I.Br See the California Standards section

COLLABORATE

Words and Categories: Describing Words Guide children to use describing words to talk about each animal: *cute, fluffy, long, short, fast, bright, soft, hard,* etc. Encourage children to add details as they draw a pet in the space provided.

Ask partners to use describing words as they tell each other about the pets they drew. See Teacher's Edition p. 489 for scaffolded support with this page.

ELD.PI.K.I.Em, ELD.PI.K.I.Ex, ELD.PI.K.I.Br;
ELD.PII.K.4.Em See the California Standards section

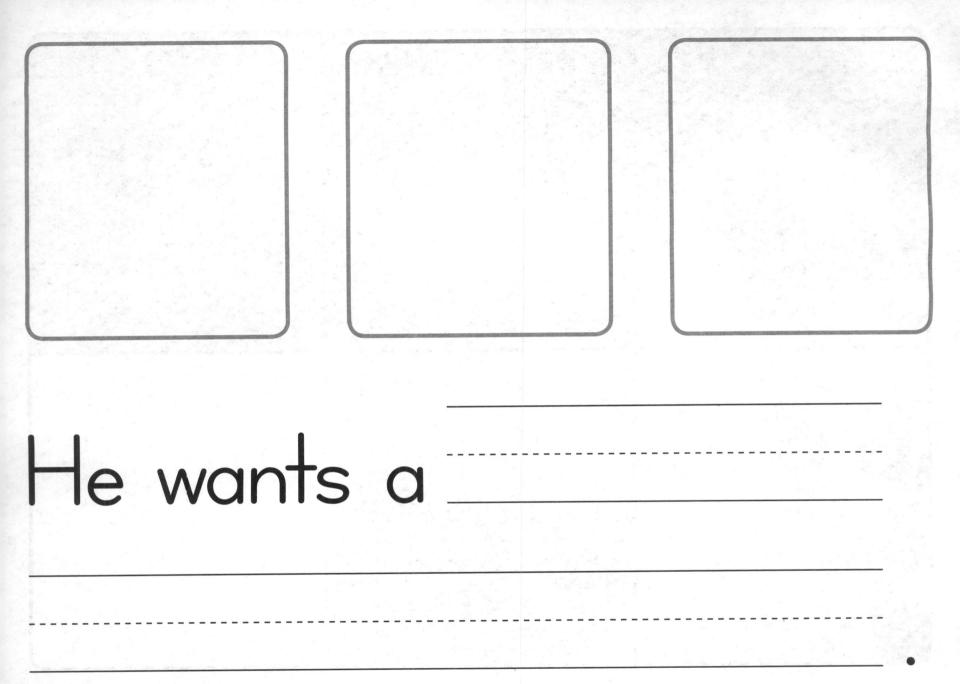

He wants a _____

_____ .

Respond to the Text: *The Birthday Pet* Review the selection, then have children draw three pets that Danny gets. Ask: *Why doesn't Danny want each of these pets? What pet does Danny want?* Guide children to complete the sentence to tell what Danny wants.

Ask partners to share their work. Ask: *What animal do you think is the best pet?* Offer a sentence frame to help children support their opinions: *I think _____ is best because _____.* See Teacher's Edition p. 492 for scaffolded support with this page.

ELD.PI.K.6.Em, ELD.PI.K.6.Ex, ELD.PI.K.6.Br; ELD.PI.K.IO.Em;
ELD.PI.K.II.Em See the California Standards section

168 Unit 7 • Week 2 • Respond to the Text: Big Book

COLLABORATE

Oral Vocabulary: Caring for a Pet Guide children to name and discuss the objects. For each object, ask: *What do you do with this? How does it help a dog?* Have children draw and label a picture of how they would use some of the objects to care for a dog.

Ask partners to explain what they're doing in their drawings, and how that is helping their dogs. See Teacher's Edition p. 496 for scaffolded support with this page.

1.

2.

3.

4.

Retell "I Hug Gus!" Review the story. Then have children use the pictures to retell it. Guide children to use the sequence words "*First, next,* and *last*" in their retelling. Ask children to circle a picture that shows how the boy feels about Gus, and explain their choice.

COLLABORATE

Have partners take turns retelling the story. Offer sentence frames for the retelling: *First, Gus _____. Next, Gus _____. Last, Gus _____.* See Teacher's Edition p. 498 for scaffolded support with this page.

ELD.PI.K.6.Em, ELD.PI.K.6.Ex, ELD.PI.K.6.Br; ELD.PI.K.12a.Em, ELD.PI.K.12a.Ex, ELD.PI.K.12a.Br; ELD.PII.K.I.Em See the California Standards section

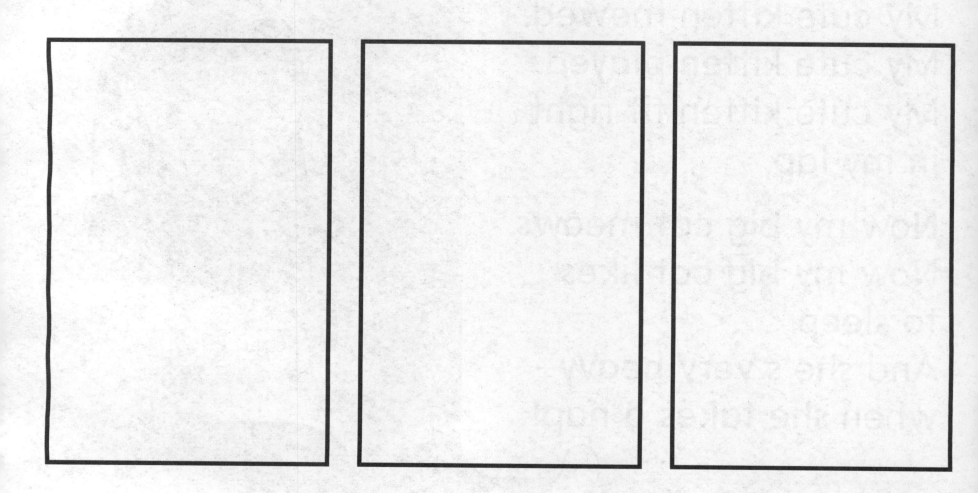

COLLABORATE

Writing Review "I Hug Gus!" Then introduce the writing prompt: *Narrate a story about the first day with a new pet.* Help children organize their ideas by drawing what happens first, next, and last in their stories. Have them label their drawings.

Ask partners to describe their drawings. Have them tell each other the story of their first day with a new pet. Encourage them to use sequence words (*first, next, then,* and *last*) and to add details. See Teacher's Edition p. 499 for scaffolded support with this page.

ELD.PI.K.6.Em; ELD.PI.K.10.Em; ELD.PII.K.I.Em
See the California Standards section

From Kitten to Cat

My cute kitten mewed.
My cute kitten played.
My cute kitten fit right
in my lap.

Now my big cat meows.
Now my big cat likes
to sleep.
And she's very heavy
when she takes a nap!

Grammar: Verbs Read the rhyme. Repeat, tracking text as children echo-read. *Guide students* to circle verbs in the first stanza. Discuss what the *-ed* ending means. Then have children circle second-stanza verbs and tell whether the action is in the past or present.

Ask partners to replace the verbs in the first line of each stanza, to tell about other things kittens and cats might do. Invite partners to read their new lines to the group. See Teacher's Edition p. 505 for scaffolded support with this page.

ELD.PI.K.5.Em, ELD.PI.K.5.Ex, ELD.PI.K.5.Br; ELD.PI.K.9.Em;
ELD.PII.K.3b.Em, ELD.PII.K.3b.Ex See the California Standards section

The Dog and the Pig

They have a lot of fun.
They run in the sun.
They are a big dog and
a little pig!

They run and they kick.
They dig and they nip.
They like to nap in mud.

COLLABORATE

Fluency Read the story. Then ask children to read it, copying your phrasing and expression. Ask: *What are the dog and pig doing?* Have children circle the weekly high-frequency words *they* and *of*.

Ask partners to take turns reading the story until they can read it fluently. Then ask them to read it in unison, remembering to pause after each sentence. See Teacher's Edition p. 506 for scaffolded support with this page.

ELD.PI.K.5.Em, ELD.PI.K.5.Ex, ELD.PI.K.5.Br;
ELD.PIII.K See the California Standards section

Weekly Concept: Animal Habitats

? Essential Question
Where do animals live?

COLLABORATE

Weekly Concept: Animal Habitats Guide children to name the animals in the picture and talk about where they live. Have children circle the parts of the picture that show an animal's home, such as the log, the underground burrow, and the pond.

Ask partners to talk about the animal homes they circled. Ask: *How the homes alike? How are they different? Why are different homes good for different animals?* See Teacher's Edition p. 510 for scaffolded support with this page.

ELD.PI.K.I.Em, ELD.PI.K.I.Ex, ELD.PI.K.I.Br See the California Standards section

1.

growl　　　squeak　　　meow　　　roar

2.

   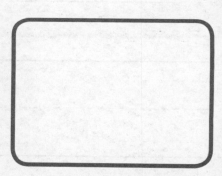

tweet　　　quack　　　oink　　　- - - - - - - - - - -

Words and Categories: Noises and Sounds Work with children to name each animal and read its sound. Children can demonstrate each sound. Ask children to draw a different animal in the empty box and label it with its sound.

Ask partners to take turns naming an animal on this page. Have them read the sound word, then imitate the animal's sound. See Teacher's Edition p. 513 for scaffolded support with this page.

ELD.PI.K.I.Em, ELD.PI.K.I.Ex, ELD.PI.K.I.Br See the California Standards section

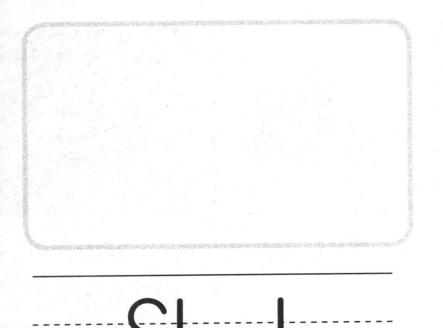

_____ Start _____   _____ End _____

_____
_____ is sleeping at the
_____
.
_____

COLLABORATE

Respond to the Text: ***Bear Snores On*** Review the book. Ask: *Who comes to Bear's den? What do they do?* Ask children to draw an animal that's sleeping at the start and end of the book, in the boxes. Then have them complete the sentence, describing one animal.

Ask partners to use their drawings and sentences to help them retell the story. See Teacher's Edition p. 516 for scaffolded support with this page.

ELD.PI.K.6.Em, ELD.PI.K.6.Ex, ELD.PI.K.6.Br; ELD.PI.K.12a.Em, ELD.PI.K.12a.Ex, ELD.PI.K.12a.Br; ELD.PII.K.2.Em See the California Standards section

1.

2.

3.

4.

Oral Vocabulary: Habitats Guide children to describe the animals and the habitats shown. Talk about why each habitat is a good home for the animal in it. Then have children draw another animal in its habitat.

Ask partners to share their drawings, describing the habitat and the animal that lives in it. *Ask: Why is that is a good home for this animal? How do you think the animal gets what it needs?* See Teacher's Edition p. 520 for scaffolded support with this page.

ELD.PI.K.I.Em, ELD.PI.K.I.Ex, ELD.PI.K.I.Br See the California Standards section

1.

2.

3.

4.

Retell: "A Vet in a Van" Review the selection. Then have children use the pictures in the correct sequence to retell the story. Provide sentence frames to guide retelling, such as: *The vet drives a _____. First, the vet _____. Next, the vet _____.*

Ask partners to take turns retelling the story to each other. Encourage them to use complete sentences and sequence words. See Teacher's Edition p. 522 for scaffolded support with this page.

ELD.PI.K.6.Em, ELD.PI.K.6.Ex, ELD.PI.K.6.Br; ELD.PI.K.I2a.Em, ELD.PI.K.I2a.Ex, ELD.PI.K.I2a.Br; ELD.PII.K.I.Em See the California Standards section

1. I like _____

_____ .

2. I don't like _____

_____ .

Writing Review "A Vet in a Van." Introduce the prompt: *Write a book report about your opinion about the art.* Talk about the art. Ask: *What do you notice? What do/don't you like?* Guide children to answer these questions orally, then complete the sentences.

ELD.PI.K.2.Em, ELD.PI.K.2.Ex; ELD.PI.K.10.Em, ELD.PI.K.10.Ex; ELD.PI.K.11.Em See the California Standards section

COLLABORATE

Ask partners to read their sentences. Then have them work together to complete this sentence in various ways: *I think the art is _____ because _____.* See Teacher's Edition p. 523 for scaffolded support with this page.

Unit 7 • Week 3 • Writing 179

Where Will They Live?

Squirrel will build his home.
She will live in a tree.
Rabbit will dig in the dirt.
He will live under me.

Bird will find sticks.
She will make a pile.
Bird will rest in her nest.
She will sing for a long while.

Grammar: Verbs Read the poem. Repeat, tracking text as children echo-read. Ask children to identify the verbs. Ask: *What changes when you add the word* will *before a verb?* Guide children to circle each pair of words that make up a future tense verb.

Ask partners to replace one of the verbs with a new verb, keeping the word *will* before it. Ask: *Does this action happen in the present or the future?* See Teacher's Edition p. 529 for scaffolded support with this page.

ELD.PI.K.5.Em, ELD.PI.K.5.Ex, ELD.PI.K.5.Br;
ELD.PII.K.3a.Em See the California Standards section

The Box

Fox and Ox can see a box.
"It is my box," said Fox.
"It is my box," said Ox.
"I want to go in," said Ox.
"You are big," said Fox.
"This box is little," said Ox.

COLLABORATE

Fluency Read the selection, modeling how to read dialogue. Then ask children to read the selection chorally, copying your phrasing. Ask: *What does the fox want? What does the ox want?* Have children circle the high-frequency words *said* and *want*.

Ask partners to take turns reading the story to each other until they can read it fluently. Ask: *Where do you pause when you're reading a sentence with quotation marks?* See Teacher's Edition p. 530 for scaffolded support with this page.

ELD.PI.K.5.Em, ELD.PI.K.5.Ex, ELD.PI.K.5.Br;
ELD.PIII.K See the California Standards section

Unit 8

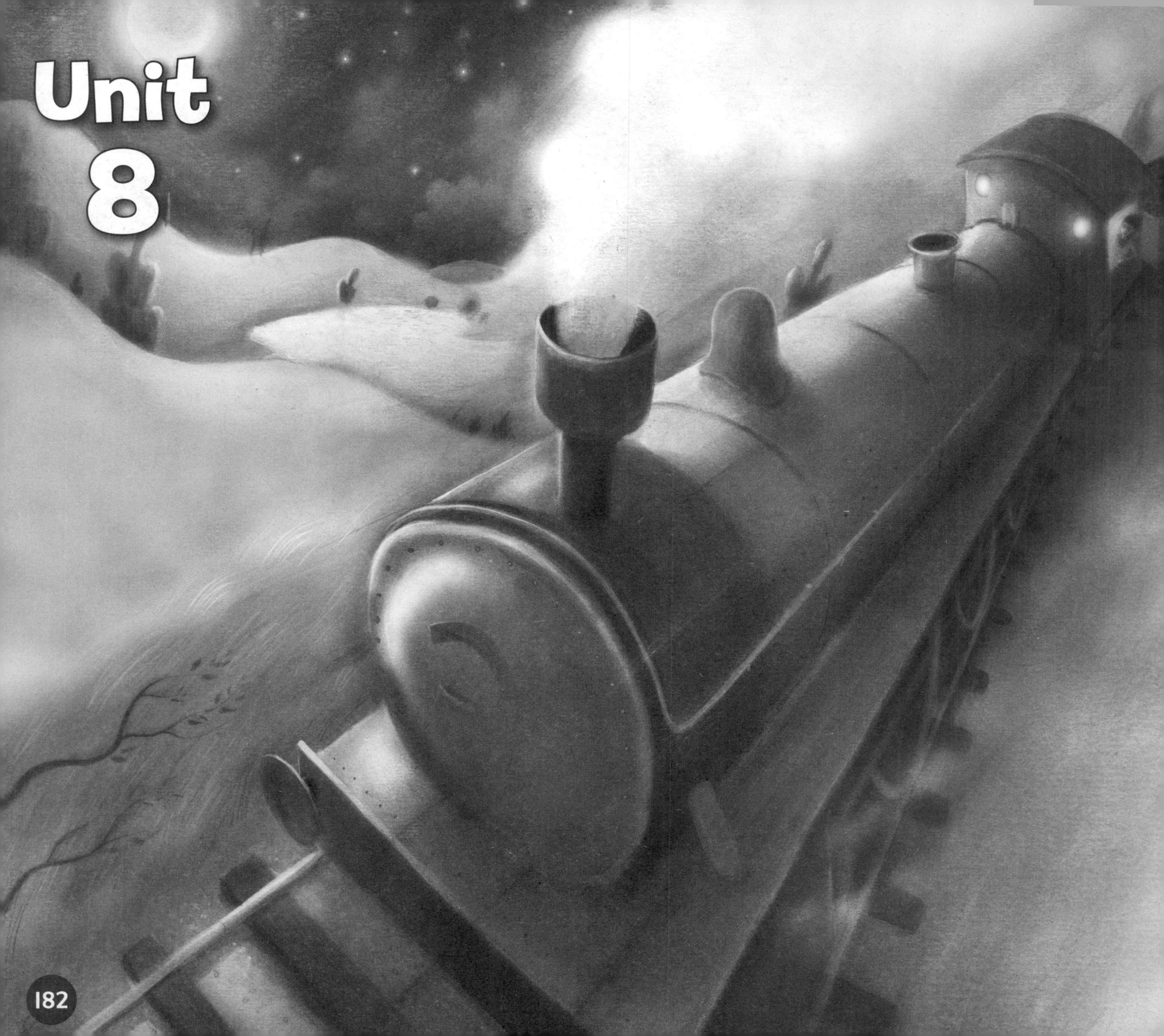

From Here to There

The Big Idea

Where can you go
that is near and far?

? **Essential Question**

What can help you go from here to there?

COLLABORATE

Weekly Concept: On the Move Guide children to talk about the four kinds of transportation shown here. Ask: *Which kinds of transportation are good for traveling far? Which are good for short trips?* Children can circle the ways they have traveled.

Ask partners to tell about a time they took a car, train, boat, or airplane. Ask: *Where did you go? How long was the trip? What did you see on the way? Describe how it felt to travel this way.* See Teacher's Edition p. 538 for scaffolded support with this page.

ELD.PI.K.I.Em, ELD.PI.K.I.Ex, ELD.PI.K.I.Br See the California Standards section

COLLABORATE

Words and Categories: Traffic Words Guide children to describe the picture. Review traffic words such as: *highway, lanes, vehicle, heavy/light traffic.* Ask: *How can you tell this is a highway? Do you think the traffic is heavy or light?* Have children draw in a vehicle.

Ask partners to share their drawings. Have them take turns using traffic words to describe their vehicle's journey. See Teacher's Edition p. 541 for scaffolded support with this page.

ELD.PI.K.I.Em, ELD.PI.K.I.Ex, ELD.PI.K.I.Br See the California Standards section

Unit 8 • Week I • Words and Categories **185**

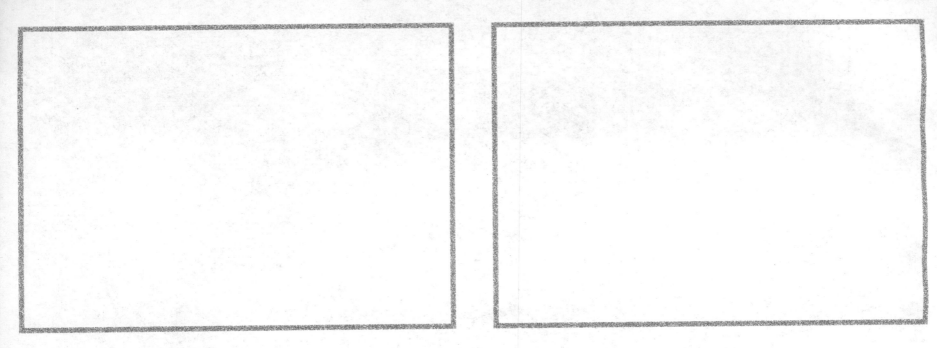

Before

After

Respond to the Text: ***When Daddy's Truck Picks Me Up*** Review the story. Guide children to draw the boy's face to show his feelings before and after his Daddy picks him up. Then have them write a sentence describing how the boy's feelings changed.

Ask partners to share their drawings and read their sentences aloud. Have them take turns asking and answering questions about the story such as: *What was the Daddy's job? Why was he late?* See Teacher's Edition p. 544 for scaffolded support with this page.

ELD.PI.K.6.Em, ELD.PI.K.6.Ex, ELD.PI.K.6.Br; ELD.PII.K.I.Em, ELD.PII.K.I.Ex See the California Standards section

COLLABORATE

Oral Vocabulary: Travel to School Guide children to describe the ways of getting to school. Ask: *Which ways use wheels? Which are good for your health? Which are better if the school is far away?* Ask children to draw the way they get to school.

Ask partners to share their drawings. Then have them tell about their trip to school this morning. See Teacher's Edition p. 548 for scaffolded support with this page.

ELD.PI.K.I.Em, ELD.PI.K.I.Ex, ELD.PI.K.I.Br See the California Standards section

1.

2.

3.

4.

Retell "Dad Got a Job" Review the story. Then ask children to retell it, using the pictures in the correct sequence. Ask questions such as: *Where is Dad's new job? How does the family get there? Do they travel a short or long distance? How do you know?*

COLLABORATE

Ask partners to take turns retelling the story, using the pictures as a guide. Offer a sentence frame: *The family took a _____ to go to _____.* See Teacher's Edition p. 548 for scaffolded support with this page.

ELD.PI.K.6.Em, ELD.PI.K.6.Ex, ELD.PI.K.6.Br; ELD.PI.K.I2a.Em, ELD.PI.K.I2a.Ex, ELD.PI.K.I2a.Br; ELD.PII.K.I.Em See the California Standards section

First	Next	Last

First, I felt _____

_____

Writing Review "Dad Got a Job." Introduce the prompt: *Write a journal entry from the girl's point of view. Tell how she feels about moving. Use first, next, and last.* Guide children to draw or write what happens first, next, and last, and complete the sentence.

ELD.PI.K.IO.Em, ELD.PI.K.IO.Ex; ELD.PII.K.I.Em
See the California Standards section

COLLABORATE

Have partners use their drawings to help them retell the story from the girl's point of view. Offer sentence frames: *First, I felt _____.* *Next, I felt _____. Last, I felt _____.* See Teacher's Edition p. 55l for scaffolded support with this page.

Unit 8 • Week I • Writing 189

Driving to Grandma's

We are driving to Grandma's.
We all sit in our seats.
I play a game with my sister
as we ride across the streets.

Our car goes over bridges.
It goes under the trees.
I can't wait to see my Grandma.
Drive faster Mommy, please!

Grammar: Sentences with Prepositions Read the rhyme. Repeat, as children echo-read. Point out the prepositional phrases in each line. Reread the rhyme, tracking the words, and ask children to clap when they hear a preposition.

Ask partners to create a sentence about traveling, using one of these prepositions: *to, of, for, from, with,* or *on*. Children can present their sentences to the group. See Teacher's Edition p. 557 for scaffolded support with this page.

ELD.PI.K.2.Em; ELD.PI.K.5.Em, ELD.PI.K.5.Ex, ELD.PI.K.5.Br; ELD.PI.K.9.Em; ELD.PII.K.5.Em, ELD.PII.K.5.Ex See the California Standards section

I Am Sick

I am here in bed.
I am sick, Mom said.
It is not fun.

I want to run.
I want to go in a jet.
I want to be quick!
I do not want to be sick!

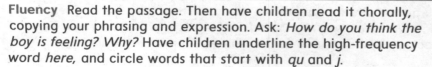

Fluency Read the passage. Then have children read it chorally, copying your phrasing and expression. Ask: *How do you think the boy is feeling? Why?* Have children underline the high-frequency word *here,* and circle words that start with *qu* and *j.*

ELD.PI.K.5.Em, ELD.PI.K.5.Ex, ELD.PI.K.5.Br; ELD.PIII.K
See the California Standards section

Ask partners to take turns reading the story to each other until they can read it fluently. Ask: *Have you ever felt like this boy? Tell about it.* See Teacher's Edition p. 558 for scaffolded support with this page.

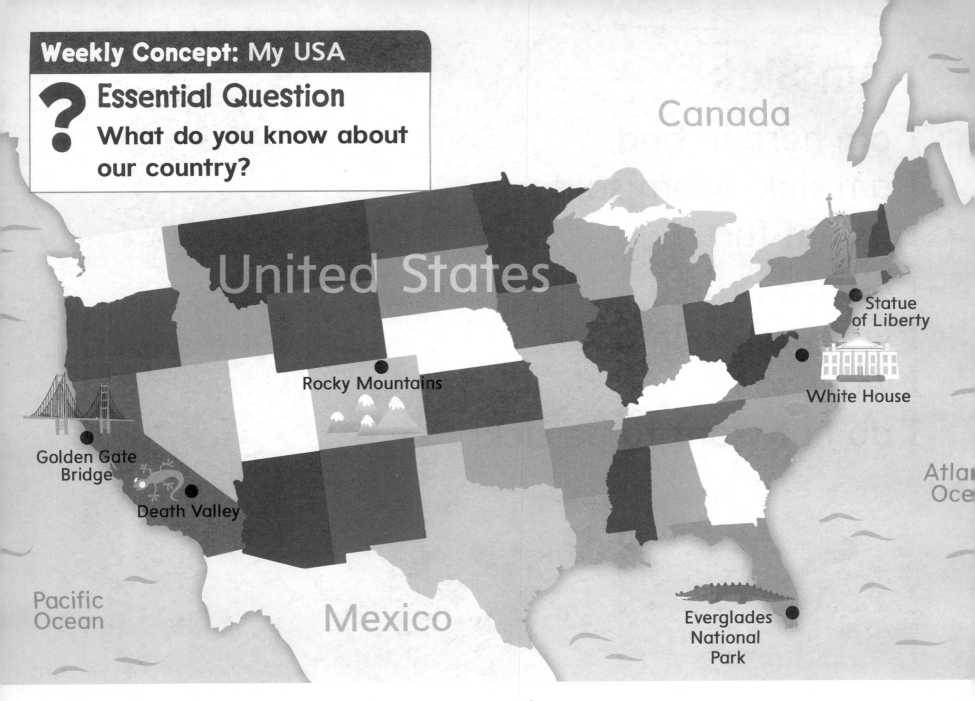

Weekly Concept: My USA

? Essential Question
What do you know about our country?

Canada

United States

Statue of Liberty

White House

Rocky Mountains

Golden Gate Bridge

Death Valley

Pacific Ocean

Mexico

Everglades National Park

Atlantic Ocean

COLLABORATE

Weekly Concept: My USA Point out the features of the map for children: landmarks, countries, states, borders, and bodies of water. Help students find your state and talk about nearby landmarks. Ask them to draw an X in the area where they live.

Ask partners to talk about the city and state they live in. Then ask: *What places in the United States would you like to visit?* See Teacher's Edition p. 562 for scaffolded support with this page.

1.

suitcase

hotel

map

tickets

2.

restaurant

tour bus

monument

Words and Categories: Traveling Point to each image and read its label. Explain that traveling is one way to learn about your country. Say: *Can you explain how each object is used while traveling? Draw another object you can use when you travel, and label it.*

COLLABORATE

Ask partners to take turns naming the objects on this page. Have them share their drawings. Ask: *How would you use your object when you travel? Explain it to your partner.* See Teacher's Edition p. 565 for scaffolded support with this page.

COLLABORATE

Respond to the Text: *Ana Goes to Washington, D.C.* Review the story, then guide children to retell it. Ask: *Where does tía Luisa take Ana and her family first? Next? Last?* Have children draw their favorite part of the story and describe it in a sentence.

Have partners share their drawings and read their sentences aloud. Ask children to tell what they like about their favorite part. See Teacher's Edition p. 568 for scaffolded support with this page.

ELD.PI.K.6.Em, ELD.PI.K.6.Ex, ELD.PI.K.6.Br; ELD.PI.K.I2a.Em,
ELD.PI.K.I2a.Ex, ELD.PI.K.I2a.Br See the California Standards section

Lincoln Memorial

Bald Eagle

Washington Monument

United States Flag

Martin Luther King, Jr. Memorial

COLLABORATE

Oral Vocabulary: U.S. Symbols Review the meaning of *symbol*. Then guide students to name and talk about each symbol on this page. Ask students to choose their favorite U.S. symbol and draw it *in the empty box.*

Ask partners to share their drawings. Have them explain why they chose the symbol they did. See Teacher's Edition p. 572 for scaffolded support with this page.

1.

2.

3.

4.

COLLABORATE

Retell "Pack a Bag!" Review the story. Then have children use the pictures in the correct sequence to retell it. Ask questions such as: *Who is Zeb going to visit? Who helps him on the plane? What do Zeb and Pop do together?*

Ask partners to take turns retelling the story. Offer sentence frames to encourage the use of full sentences: *The boy is going _____. _____ helps the boy _____. Zeb and Pop _____.* See Teacher's Edition p. 574 for scaffolded support with this page.

ELD.PI.K.6.Em, ELD.PI.K.6.Ex, ELD.PI.K.6.Br; ELD.PI.K.12a.Em, ELD.PI.K.12a.Ex, ELD.PI.K.12a.Br See the California Standards section

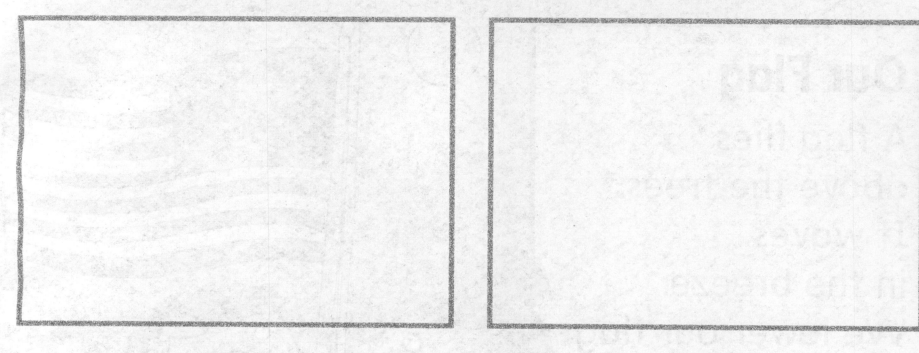

Clue

Clue

One clue is _____

_____

_____

•

Writing Review "Pack a Bag!" Then, introduce the prompt: *How do the author and illustrator show you that Zeb enjoyed his trip?* Have children draw or write two clues that show Zeb enjoyed his trip. Then have them complete the sentence.

ELD.PI.K.6.Em, ELD.PI.K.6.Ex, ELD.PI.K.6.Br; ELD.PI.K.IO.Em, ELD.PI.K.IO.Ex See the California Standards section

Ask partners to describe the clues they found, and read their sentences aloud. Children can address the prompt orally: *The author and illustrator show me that Zeb enjoyed his trip by* _____ . See Teacher's Edition p. 575 for scaffolded support with this page.

Unit 8 • Week 2 • Writing **197**

Our Flag

A flag flies
above the trees.
It waves
in the breeze.
We lower our flag
at night.
Then we raise it
in sunlight.

COLLABORATE

Grammar: Sentences with Prepositions Read the rhyme. Then reread it, as children echo-read. Point out the prepositions. Ask: *What do the prepositions in each sentence tell you?* Read the rhyme once more, tracking the words, and ask children to underline each preposition.

Choose an object in the classroom. Ask partners to use several prepositions to describe its location. (E.g. *It is above the board/near the door*, etc.). See Teacher's Edition p. 58I for scaffolded support with this page.

ELD.PI.K.5.Em, ELD.PI.K.5.Ex, ELD.PI.K.5.Br; ELD.PII.K.5.Em, ELD.PII.K.5.Ex See the California Standards section

I Am Zip

I am Zip.
This is what I can do.
Can I zig? Yes!
Can I zag? Yes!
I can zip, zip, zip.
Look up!
What can you see?
It is me!

Fluency Read the story, modeling the intonation used for questions and exclamations. Then reread as children echo-read, copying your intonation. Have children underline the high-frequency words *this* and *what* and circle words that start with *y* or *z*.

Ask partners to take turns reading the story to each other until they can read it fluently. Say: *Read the last sentence. Then pretend that sentence ends in a period. How would you read it now?* See Teacher's Edition p. 582 for scaffolded support with this page.

ELD.PI.K.5.Em, ELD.PI.K.5.Ex, ELD.PI.K.5.Br; ELD.PIII.K
See the California Standards section

Weekly Concept: Look to the Sky

? **Essential Question**

What do you see in the sky?

COLLABORATE

Weekly Concept: Look to the Sky Guide children to name the objects in the sky. Talk about the time of day shown (twilight). Ask: *What can we see in the sky in the daytime? Nighttime? Twilight?* Have children draw something else they could see in the sky.

Have partners describe their drawings. Then ask them to look out the classroom window and talk about what they see in the sky. See Teacher's Edition p. 586 for scaffolded support with this page.

ELD.PI.K.I.Em, ELD.PI.K.I.Ex, ELD.PI.K.I.Br See the California Standards section

1.

night close bright high

2.

far dark day low

COLLABORATE

Words and Categories: Opposites Read the labels as children repeat. Guide them to explain what each word means. Review the definition of *opposites*. Work together to match one set of opposites (e.g. *night/day*), then ask children to match the other sets.

Ask partners to take turns naming sets of opposites. Provide starter words such as *tall, loud, thick, pull, sweet,* or *dry* as needed. See Teacher's Edition p. 589 for scaffolded support with this page.

COLLABORATE

Respond to the Text: ***Bringing Down the Moon*** Review the story. Have children use the pictures to describe ways Mole tries to bring down the moon. Ask: *What does Mole learn?* Then ask children to draw a picture that shows the end of the story, and write about it.

Ask partners to talk about their drawings and read their writing aloud. Then have them work together to explain how the different characters help Mole. See Teacher's Edition p. 592 for scaffolded support with this page.

ELD.PI.K.6.Em, ELD.PI.K.6.Ex, ELD.PI.K.6.Br; ELD.PI.K.I2a.Em, ELD.PI.K.I2a.Ex, ELD.PI.K.I2a.Br See the California Standards section

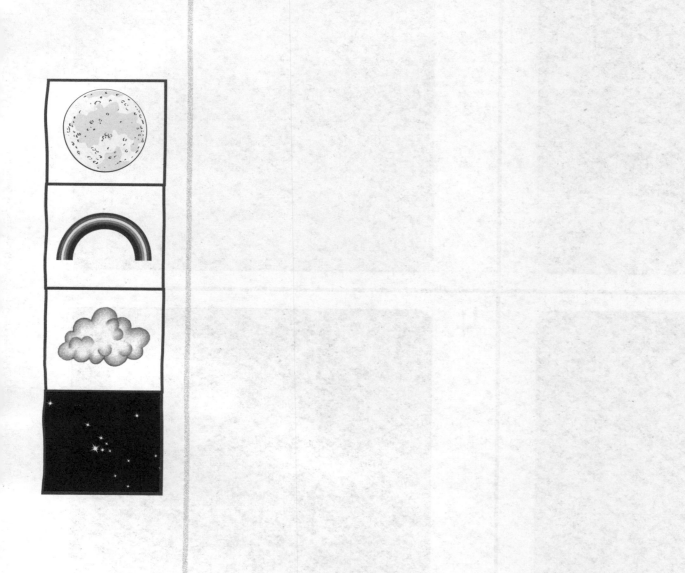

Oral Vocabulary: **Objects in the Sky** Guide children to describe the pictures. Ask: *What objects have you observed in the sky? What time of day did you see them?* Have children draw a daytime or nighttime sky that includes several of the objects pictured.

Ask partners to share their drawings and talk about the objects they included. See Teacher's Edition p. 596 for scaffolded support with this page.

ELD.PI.K.I.Em, ELD.PI.K.I.Ex, ELD.PI.K.I.Br See the California Standards section

1.

2.

3.

4.

(tl) Photo Researchers/Getty Images; (tr) Photodisc/Eyewire/Getty Images; (bl) ; (br) Corbis RF

Retell "Up, Up, Up!" Review the story. Then ask children to describe what the scientist sees. Ask questions such as: *How does the telescope help the scientist observe objects? What would you like to see through a telescope?*

Ask partners to point to the pictures, naming the objects. Then, have partners share their favorite things to observe in the sky. See Teacher's Edition p. 598 for scaffolded support with this page.

204 Unit 8 • Week 3 • Retell: Shared Read

ELD.PI.K.6.Em, ELD.PI.K.6.Ex, ELD.PI.K.6.Br See the California Standards section

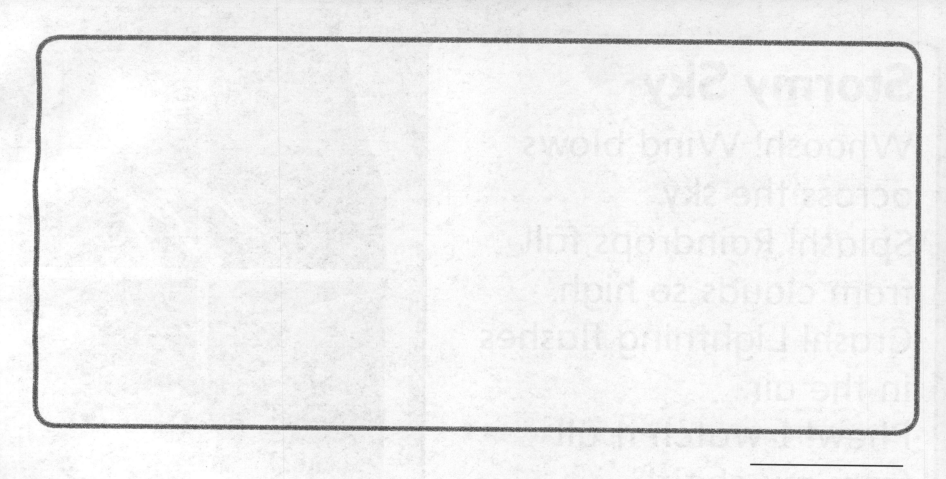

He's in luck because

Writing Review "Up! Up! Up!" Introduce the prompt: *Why does the narrator think that he's "in luck"? How can you tell?* Ask children to draw an image from the book that helps to show why the narrator feels lucky. Then have them complete the sentence to explain it.

Ask partners to share their work. Review the writing prompt. Have partners use these sentence frames to talk about it: *The narrator thinks that he's in luck because _____. I can tell by _____.* See Teacher's Edition p. 599 for scaffolded support with this page.

ELD.PI.K.6.Em, ELD.PI.K.6.Ex, ELD.PI.K.6.Br; ELD.PI.K.IO.Em, ELD.PI.K.IO.Ex See the California Standards section

Stormy Sky

Whoosh! Wind blows
across the sky.
Splash! Raindrops fall
from clouds so high.
Crash! Lightning flashes
in the air.
Phew! I watch it all
from my chair!

Grammar: Sentences with Prepositions Read the rhyme. Reread it, as children echo-read. Remind children that prepositions can help to tell where, when, or how something happens. Then guide children to underline the prepositions in the rhyme.

Have partners replace one of the prepositions in the rhyme with a different preposition. Ask: *How did that change the meaning of the sentence?* See Teacher's Edition p. 605 for scaffolded support with this page.

ELD.PI.K.2.Em; ELD.PI.K.5.Em, ELD.PI.K.5.Ex, ELD.PI.K.5.Br; ELD.PII.K.5.Em See the California Standards section

The Sun Is Up

"I am up," said the Sun.
"It is hot, hot, hot.
Can you see me up here?
I like this job a lot!
Do I have to set?
I do not want to quit yet!"

Fluency Read the rhyme, pointing out how your voice changes for questions and exclamations. Have children read the rhyme chorally, copying your intonation and expression. Then ask them to underline the high-frequency words *want, this, me,* and *here.*

COLLABORATE

Ask partners to take turns reading the rhyme to each other until they can read it fluently. Ask: *What is the Sun saying in the poem? What does the Sun want?* See Teacher's Edition p. 606 for more work with this page.

ELD.PI.K.5.Em, ELD.PI.K.5.Ex, ELD.PI.K.5.Br; ELD.PIII.K
See the California Standards section

How Things Change

The Big Idea

How do things change?

? **Essential Question**

How can you help out at home?

COLLABORATE

Weekly Concept: Growing Up Guide children to describe the picture. Ask: *How are each of the children helping? How do you help at home?* Have children circle jobs that they have done. Then have them draw themselves helping in the kitchen.

Ask partners to tell about ways that they help at home. Ask: *Can you think of other ways you would like to help?* See Teacher's Edition p. 614 for scaffolded support with this page.

210 Unit 9 • Week I • Weekly Concept

ELD.PI.K.I.Em, ELD.PI.K.I.Ex, ELD.PI.K.I.Br See the California Standards section

Words and Categories: Helping with a Baby Guide children to talk about how a baby uses each object. Ask: *What else could help a baby stay safe and happy? Draw one object.* (E.g. a car seat, clothing, or toys.) Ask: *How could you help to care for a baby?*

Ask partners to take turns naming the objects on this page. Then have them share their drawings. Ask: *How would you use this object to take care of a baby?* See Teacher's Edition p. 617 for scaffolded support with this page.

ELD.PI.K.I.Em, ELD.PI.K.I.Ex, ELD.PI.K.I.Br See the California Standards section

First, Peter

Last, Peter

Respond to the Text: *Peter's Chair* Review the book. Then guide children to retell the story. Ask: *What did Peter see at his house? What did Peter do first? What happened next? What happened at the end?* Have children write about what happened first and last.

Invite partners to read their sentences to each other. Then ask them to describe Peter's feelings at the beginning, middle, and end of the story. See Teacher's Edition p. 620 for scaffolded support with this page.

ELD.PI.K.6.Em, ELD.PI.K.6.Ex, ELD.PI.K.6.Br; ELD.PI.K.I2a.Em, ELD.PI.K.I2a.Ex, ELD.PI.K.I2a.Br; ELD.PII.K.2.Em See the California Standards section

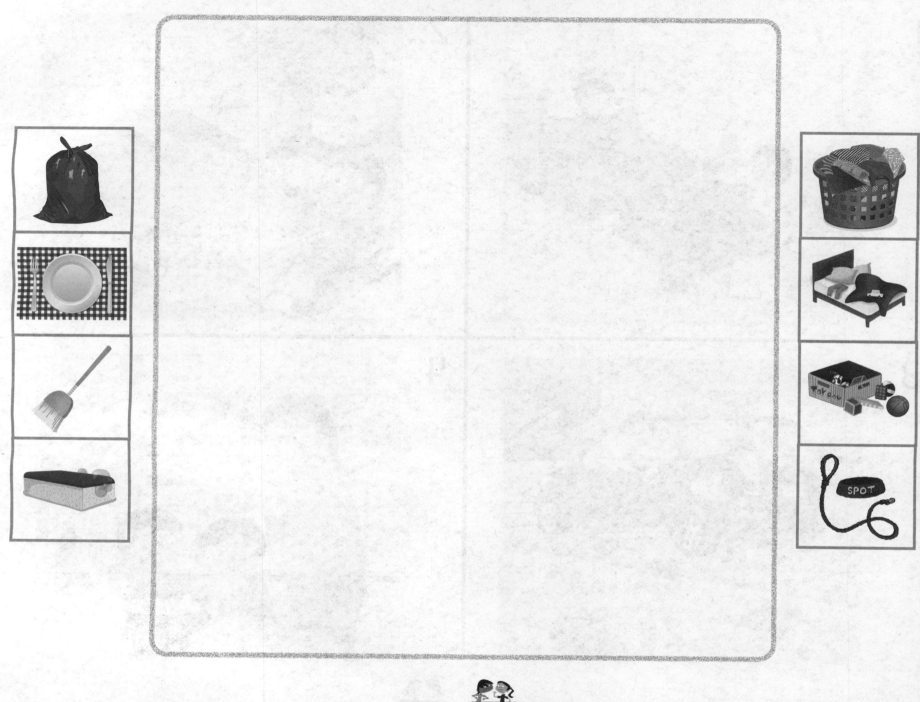

Oral Vocabulary: Jobs Around the House Guide children to name the objects. For each object, ask: *What job could this help you do?* Guide children to pair verbs and nouns: *wash the floor, set the table, etc.* Have children draw themselves using one of the objects.

Invite partners to describe their drawings. Ask: *How does it help your family when you do this job?* See Teacher's Edition p. 624 for scaffolded support with this page.

1.

2.

3.

4.

Retell "Jake and Dale Help!" Review the story. Then ask children to retell it, using the pictures as a guide. Ask: *How do the boys help at home? How do the boys help when they go out?*

Have partners take turns retelling the story. Ask: *How do you think Jake, Dale, Mom, and Dad feel? What clues help you know this?* See Teacher's Edition p. 626 for scaffolded support with this page.

ELD.PI.K.6.Em, ELD.PI.K.6.Ex, ELD.PI.K.6.Br; ELD.PI.K.12a.Em, ELD.PI.K.12a.Ex, ELD.PI.K.12a.Br See the California Standards section

I felt

_____

- -

_____

_____

- -

_____ .

COLLABORATE

Writing Review "Jake and Dale Help!" Introduce the prompt: _Write a journal entry as Dad describing how he felt about how Dale and Jake helped._ Have children draw Jake and Dale helping Dad. Then have them complete the sentence to describe how Dad felt.

Have partners share their drawing and writing. Ask them to find more than one way to describe Dad's feelings. Offer a choice of adjectives: _happy, surprised, pleased, proud, thankful, angry, cheerful._ See Teacher's Edition p. 627 for scaffolded support with this page.

ELD.PI.K.6.Em, ELD.PI.K.6.Ex, ELD.PI.K.6.Br; ELD.PI.K.IO.Em, ELD.PI.K.IO.Ex See the California Standards section

Nate Helps

Nate is a helpful boy.
He cleans a messy room.
He picks up a red toy
and a scary costume.

After his room is neat,
he gets into his soft bed.
He pulls back the sheet,
and rests his tired head.

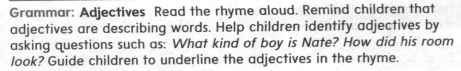

Grammar: Adjectives Read the rhyme aloud. Remind children that adjectives are describing words. Help children identify adjectives by asking questions such as: *What kind of boy is Nate? How did his room look?* Guide children to underline the adjectives in the rhyme.

Ask partners to draw a real or imaginary bedroom, and list adjectives that describe it. You can offer a starter list with words such as: *green, small, nice, messy, neat, bright.* See Teacher's Edition p. 633 for scaffolded support with this page.

ELD.PI.K.2.Em; ELD.PI.K.5.Em, ELD.PI.K.5.Ex, ELD.PI.K.5.Br; ELD.PII.K.4.Em See the California Standards section

Jane Can Help, Too

Dad got this on sale.
He can fix it.
He can make it safe.

Can Jane help too?
Yes! She can help Dad.
Jane and Dad can do it!

Fluency Track the text as you read the passage. Then reread it as children echo-read, copying your expression and phrasing. Have children underline the high-frequency words *help* and *too*, and circle words that have the long *a* sound.

ELD.PI.K.5.Em, ELD.PI.K.5.Ex, ELD.PI.K.5.Br; ELD.PIII.K See the California Standards section

COLLABORATE

Ask partners to take turns reading the passage until they can read it fluently. Then have them explain what Jane and Dad are doing, in their own words. See Teacher's Edition p. 634 for scaffolded support with this page.

Weekly Concept: Good Citizens

? Essential Question
What do good citizens do?

COLLABORATE

Weekly Concept: Good Citizens Ask children to find the good citizens in the picture, and describe what each one is doing. (For example: *The girl is waiting her turn at the water fountain.*) Have children circle the ways that they would like to be good citizens.

Ask partners to describe the good citizens they circled. Then ask them to think of other ways to be good citizens at school. See Teacher's Edition p. 638 for scaffolded support with this page.

218 Unit 9 • Week 2 • Weekly Concept

ELD.PI.K.I.Em, ELD.PI.K.I.Ex, ELD.PI.K.I.Br See the California Standards section

COLLABORATE

Words and Categories: Farm Animals Guide children to name the animals and share what they know about them. For example: *Hens lay eggs; cows give milk.* Have children draw a farm scene with some of the animals from the picture bank, and add labels.

Partners can take turns naming the animals at the bottom of the page. Then ask them to describe their drawings to each other. See Teacher's Edition p. 641 for scaffolded support with this page.

1.

2.

3.

The animals think _____

_____

•

_____

Respond to the Text: *Hen Hears Gossip* Review the story. Ask: *What do the animals think happened? Are they correct? What really happened? Why were the animals wrong?* Ask children to draw three things the animals think happens, then write about one of them.

COLLABORATE

Have partners take turns retelling the story, using their pictures as a guide. Then ask them to discuss these questions: *Is gossip always true? How do you know?* See Teacher's Edition p. 644 for scaffolded support with this page.

ELD.PI.K.6.Em, ELD.PI.K.6.Ex, ELD.PI.K.6.Br; ELD.PI.K.12a.Em, ELD.PI.K.12a.Ex, ELD.PI.K.12a.Br See the California Standards section

1.

2.

3.

4.

COLLABORATE

Oral Vocabulary: Being a Good Citizen Guide children to describe each scene. Ask: *Which picture shows people taking turns? Sharing? Comforting a friend?* Have children draw another way they can be good citizens when playing with a friend.

Ask partners to share their drawings and explain how they are being good citizens. Partners can act out each scene. See Teacher's Edition p. 648 for scaffolded support with this page.

ELD.PI.K.I.Em, ELD.PI.K.I.Ex, ELD.PI.K.I.Br See the California Standards section

1.

2.

3.

4.

COLLABORATE

Retell "We Can Play" Review the story. Then ask children to use the pictures to retell it. Ask questions such as: *How are the characters being good citizens? Who invites a friend to play?*

Invite partners to take turns pointing to a person in a picture, and asking: *How is she/he being a good citizen?* Have the other partner answer using a complete sentence. See Teacher's Edition p. 650 for scaffolded support with this page.

ELD.PI.K.6.Em, ELD.PI.K.6.Ex, ELD.PI.K.6.Br; ELD.PI.K.12a.Em, ELD.PI.K.12a.Ex, ELD.PI.K.12a.Br See the California Standards section

1. _____

   _____

2. _____

Writing Review "We Can Play." Then introduce the prompt: *Describe how the children in this story play together. Are they good citizens? Why or why not?* Have children draw two characters from the book, and describe two ways that they play together.

Ask partners to share their work. Then have them discuss whether they think the children are good citizens, and why. Offer a sentence frame: *I think the children are/aren't good citizens because _____.* See Teacher's Edition p. 651 for scaffolded support with this page.

ELD.PI.K.6.Em, ELD.PI.K.6.Ex, ELD.PI.K.6.Br; ELD.PI.K.10.Em, ELD.PI.K.10.Ex; ELD.PI.K.11.Em, ELD.PI.K.11.Ex See the California Standards section

My Helpful Friend

You are nice.
You are fair.
You are helpful.
You like to share.

You share with me.
And I share with you.
You are my friend.
And I am your friend too!

Grammar: Adjectives Read the rhyme. Repeat, as children echo-read. Have children help you identify the describing words and underline them. Then read the rhyme together and ask children to clap when they say each describing word.

Ask partners to create a list of adjectives that describes a friend. Children can start with adjectives from the poem (*nice, fair, helpful*) and add to it (*friendly, fun, clever, kind,* for example). See Teacher's Edition p. 657 for scaffolded support with this page.

ELD.PI.K.2.Em; ELD.PI.K.5.Em, ELD.PI.K.5.Ex, ELD.PI.K.5.Br; ELD.PII.K.4.Em See the California Standards section

Mike Has a Bike

Mike has a red bike.
The bike is fun to ride.
Abe and Gus want to play.
"It is mine," says Mike.
"But you can ride."
Go, Abe!
Go, Gus!
Go, Mike!

COLLABORATE

Fluency Read the selection. Then ask children to read it chorally, copying your intonation and phrasing. Ask: *What does Mike do? Is he being a good citizen?* Have children underline the high-frequency words *has* and *play* and circle the words with the long *i* sound.

ELD.PI.K.5.Em, ELD.PI.K.5.Ex, ELD.PI.K.5.Br;
ELD.PIII.K See the California Standards section

Ask partners to take turns reading the passage to each other until they can read it fluently. Remind them to pause for commas, and at the ends of sentences. See Teacher's Edition p. 658 for scaffolded support with this page.

Weekly Concept: Our Natural Resources

? Essential Question

How can things in nature be used to make new things?

Weekly Concept: Our Natural Resources Guide children to describe the picture. Ask: *What things in the picture are made from something in nature?* Then have children circle natural things that people can use (fish, trees, water).

Have partners describe the items they circled, and explain how people could make use of them. For example: *People could use water to drink; People could use fish to eat.* See Teacher's Edition p. 662 for scaffolded support with this page.

COLLABORATE

226 Unit 9 • Week 3 • Weekly Concept

ELD.PI.K.I.Em, ELD.PI.K.I.Ex, ELD.PI.K.I.Br See the California Standards section

1.

| wheat shafts | grains | grind | flour |

2.

| dough | knead | bake | bread |

COLLABORATE

Words and Categories: Making Bread Point to the pictures as you read the labels. Explain that each picture shows a step for making bread. Ask children to describe the steps. Then have them draw the finished product in the last box.

Ask partners to take turns describing the steps for making bread from wheat. Then have them share their drawings, and talk about the kinds of bread they like to eat. See Teacher's Edition p. 665 for scaffolded support with this page.

Steps for Making Bread

1. _____

2. _____

3. _____

Respond to the Text: *Bread Comes to Life* Review the book. Guide children to use the pictures to retell it. Remind them to use sequence words such as *first, next, then,* and *last.* Ask: *What are the steps for making bread?* Have children list three steps on the lines above.

Ask partners to compare their lists. Then have them work together to create a more-complete list. See Teacher's Edition p. 668 for scaffolded support with this page.

ELD.PI.K.2.Em; ELD.PI.K.6.Em, ELD.PI.K.6.Ex, ELD.PI.K.6.Br; ELD.PI.K.I2a.Em, ELD.PI.K.I2a.Ex, ELD.PI.K.I2a.Br See the California Standards section

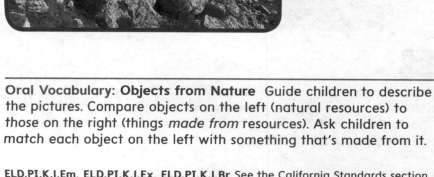

(tr) Anton Prado Photography/iStock/Getty Images Plus/Getty Images; (tcr) Ingram Publishing; (bcr) Ingram Publishing; (br) Joe Polillio/McGraw-Hill Education

Oral Vocabulary: Objects from Nature Guide children to describe the pictures. Compare objects on the left (natural resources) to those on the right (things *made from* resources). Ask children to match each object on the left with something that's made from it.

Ask children to compare their matches with a partner's. Then ask: *How do you think the resources are made into the objects? Talk about your ideas.* See Teacher's Edition p. 672 for scaffolded support with this page.

1.

2.

3.

4.

COLLABORATE

Retell "Look! A Home!" Review the book with children. Have them look at the pictures and talk about the homes. Ask questions such as: *What is the home made from? Who lives in this home?*

Have partners choose two homes on this page to compare and contrast. Ask: *How are these homes alike? How are they different? Who could live in these homes?* See Teacher's Edition p. 674 for scaffolded support with this page.

ELD.PI.K.6.Em, ELD.PI.K.6.Ex, ELD.PI.K.6.Br See the California Standards section

The homes are alike

_____

_____

_____

_____ •

Writing Review "Look! A Home!" Introduce the prompt: _Write a journal entry from the girl's point of view. Tell how the homes on pp. 38, 41, and 42 are alike and different._ Compare/contrast the homes as a group. Then ask children to write about ways they are alike.

ELD.PI.K.6.Em, ELD.PI.K.6.Ex, ELD.PI.K.6.Br; ELD.PI.K.10.Em, ELD.PI.K.10.Ex See the California Standards section

COLLABORATE

Ask partners to share their writing. Then have them practice answering the prompt orally: _The homes are alike because _____. The homes are different because _____._ See Teacher's Edition p. 675 for scaffolded support with this page.

Nature's Treats

Milk is white and cold.
Fresh bread is yummy.
A sweet green apple
fills my hungry tummy.

Nature gives delicious foods.
We make tasty snacks.
We pack healthy lunches
inside small brown sacks.

Grammar: Adjectives Read the rhyme. Repeat, as children echo-read. Ask: *Which words are describing words? Which words are the things being described?* Guide children to underline the describing words in each sentence, and circle the things being described.

Ask each child to choose a favorite lunchtime food. Then have partners create lists of adjectives that describe their favorite foods. Have them choose one adjective and use it in a sentence. See Teacher's Edition p. 681 for scaffolded support with this page.

ELD.PI.K.2.Em, ELD.PI.K.2.Ex; ELD.PI.K.5.Em, ELD.PI.K.5.Ex,
ELD.PI.K.5.Br; ELD.PII.K.4.Em See the California Standards section

232 Unit 9 • Week 3 • Grammar

Poke and His Nose

Poke had a bone.
Poke dug a hole.
Where is the bone?
Where did it go?
Poke has a nose.
Look! This nose can help.
Poke can get the bone!

Unit 10

Thinking Outside the Box

The Big Idea

How can new ideas help us?

Weekly Concept: Problem Solvers

? Essential Question

What can happen when we work together?

COLLABORATE

Weekly Concept: Problem Solvers Guide children to talk about the picture. Ask: *What are the children doing? How are they working together? What would you do to help?* Have students draw themselves helping the children build.

Ask partners to share their drawings. Then have them imagine they were building with blocks. Ask: *What will you make together? Draw a picture of what you will build.* See Teacher's Edition p. 690 for scaffolded support with this page.

ELD.PI.K.I.Em, ELD.PI.K.I.Ex, ELD.PI.K.I.Br See the California Standards section

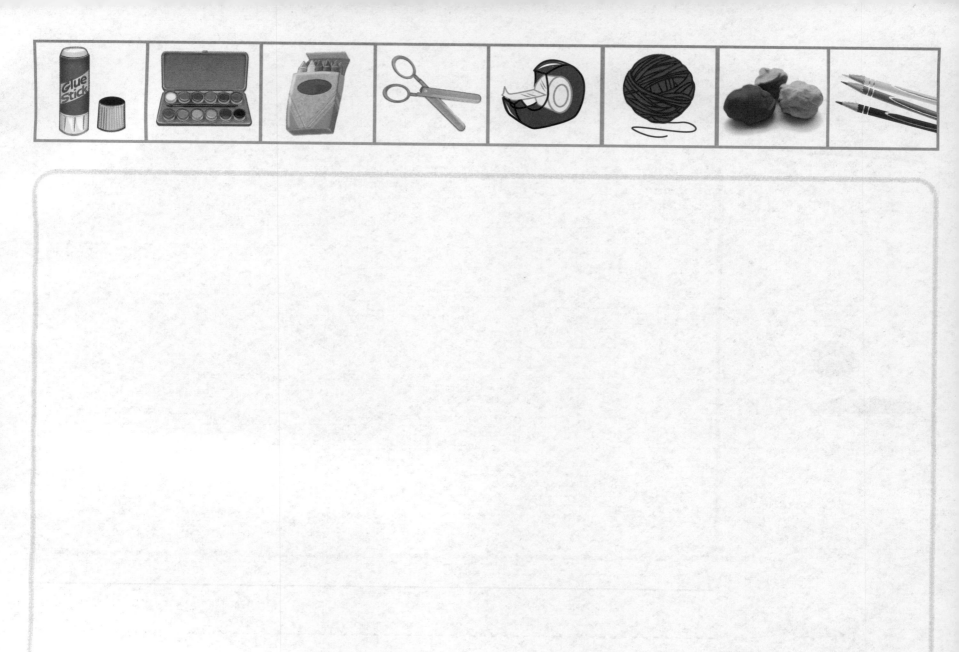

COLLABORATE

Words and Categories: Art Supplies Guide children to talk about each art supply shown. Ask: *What is this called? How do you use it? What can you make with it?* Have children draw themselves using some of the supplies.

Ask partners to describe their drawings. Then have them take turns pointing to an art supply and asking: *What is this?* Have the other partner answer using a complete sentence: *This is a _____.* See Teacher's Edition p. 693 for scaffolded support with this page.

ELD.PI.K.I.Em, ELD.PI.K.I.Ex, ELD.PI.K.I.Br See the California Standards section

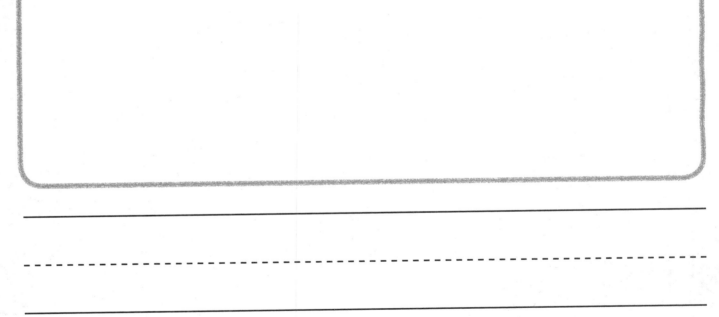

COLLABORATE

Respond to the Text: *What's the Big Idea, Molly?* Review the story. Then ask children to retell it, using the pictures as a guide. Ask: *How do the animals work together? What does each animal make?* Have children draw a picture for Turtle and write a sentence about it.

Ask partners to take turns retelling the story. Then have children share their drawing and writing. Ask: *What could you make for Turtle if you worked together?* See Teacher's Edition p. 696 for scaffolded support with this page.

ELD.PI.K.6.Em, ELD.PI.K.6.Ex, ELD.PI.K.6.Br; ELD.PI.K.10.Em; ELD.PI.K.12a.Em, ELD.PI.K.12a.Ex, ELD.PI.K.12a.Br See the California Standards section

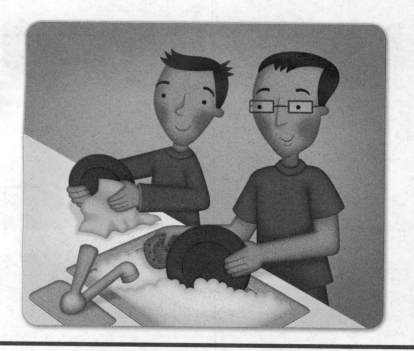

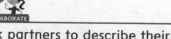

Oral Vocabulary: Cooperation Define *cooperation*. Then guide children to describe how people are cooperating in each illustration. Ask: *What are they trying to do? How are they helping each other?* Have children draw people cooperating to complete a job.

Ask partners to describe their drawings. Ask: *What job are people trying to do in your drawing? How are they cooperating?* See Teacher's Edition p. 700 for scaffolded support with this page.

1.

2.

3.

4.

COLLABORATE

Retell "A Good Time for Luke" Review the story. Then ask children to look at the pictures in sequence as they retell it. Guide children with questions such as: *What are the children planning? What steps do they take to plan the party? What kind of party is it?*

Ask partners to use sequence words as they retell the story to each other: *First the children _____. Next, they _____. Last, they _____.* See Teacher's Edition p. 702 for scaffolded support with this page.

ELD.PI.K.6.Em, ELD.PI.K.6.Ex, ELD.PI.K.6.Br; ELD.PI.K.I2a.Em, ELD.PI.K.I2a.Ex, ELD.PI.K.I2a.Br; ELD.PII.K.I.Em See the California standards section

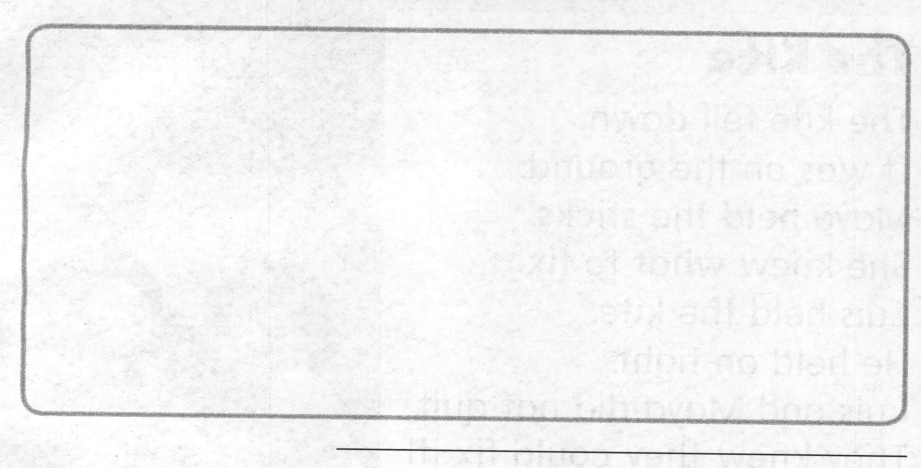

They will _____

_____

_____

_____

COLLABORATE

Writing Review "A Good Time for Luke." Then, introduce the writing prompt: *Write another story about the children celebrating the end of the school year.* Guide children to draw one way the children will celebrate, then describe it in a sentence.

ELD.PI.K.2.Em; ELD.PI.K.10.Em, ELD.PI.K.10.Ex
See the California Standards section

Have partners describe their drawings and read their sentences aloud. Ask: *Can you think of other ways the children could celebrate? Make a list of ideas.* See Teacher's Edition p. 703 for scaffolded support with this page.

The Kite

The kite fell down.
It was on the ground.
Maya held the sticks.
She knew what to fix.
Luis held the kite.
He held on tight.
Luis and Maya did not quit.
They knew they could fix it!

Grammar *Pronouns* Read the rhyme. Reread it, as children echo-read. Remind children that pronouns take the place of naming words. Reread again, tracking the words. Pause at each pronoun and ask: *Which naming word does this pronoun stand for?*

Ask partners to match each noun in the rhyme to a pronoun. Say: *Circle the pronouns in the poem. Underline the nouns that they stand for. Draw a line to connect them.* See Teacher's Edition p. 709 for scaffolded support with this page.

ELD.PI.K.5.Em, ELD.PI.K.5.Ex, ELD.PI.K.5.Br See the California Standards section

Play a Tune

We can play a tune!
Pat can use a tube.
Who can tap a box?
June can!
And Jim can use a jug.
What a good tune!

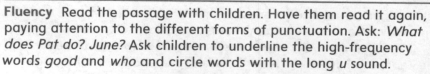

Fluency Read the passage with children. Have them read it again, paying attention to the different forms of punctuation. Ask: *What does Pat do? June?* Ask children to underline the high-frequency words *good* and *who* and circle words with the long *u* sound.

Ask partners to take turns reading the passage until they can read it fluently. Have children explain to each other how periods, question marks, and exclamation marks affect the way they read. See Teacher's Edition p. 710 for scaffolded support with this page.

ELD.PI.K.5.Em, ELD.PI.K.5.Ex, ELD.PI.K.5.Br; ELD.PIII.K
See the California Standards section

Unit 10 • Week 1 • Fluency **243**

Weekly Concept: Sort It Out

? Essential Question

In what ways are things alike?
How are they different?

COLLABORATE

Weekly Concept: Sort It Out Name the kitchen tools. Talk about ways you could sort them. Ask: *Where can you see circles? Rectangles? Which tools are used to measure? Which are made of wood?* Have children sort the tools.

Ask partners to take turns guessing how their partner sorted the tools. Have them use this frame to ask questions: *Did you sort by _____ ? (e.g. Did you sort by shape/material/what they're use for?)* See Teacher's Edition p. 714 for scaffolded support with this page.

ELD.PI.K.I.Em, ELD.PI.K.I.Ex, ELD.PI.K.I.Br See the California Standards section

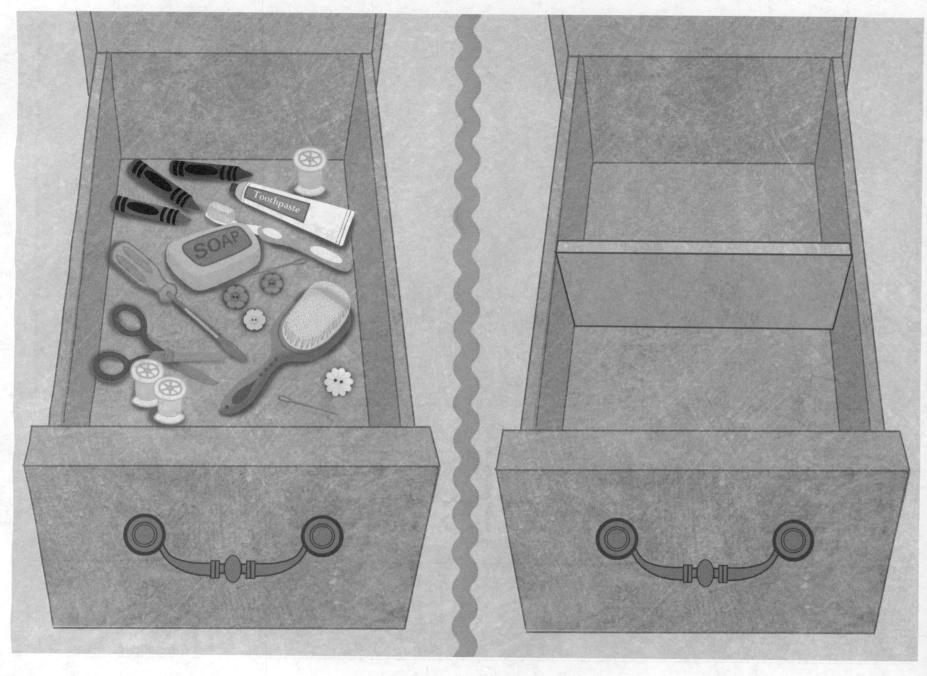

Words and Categories: Creating Categories Talk about the objects. Ask: *Which are for making art? Which help you care for your body?* Have children choose two categories. Then have them draw their two categories of objects on the right.

Ask partners to share their drawings and describe how they sorted their objects. Offer this sentence frame: *These objects are similar because* _____. See Teacher's Edition p. 717 for scaffolded support with this page.

[blank drawing box]

These objects are ____

____

Respond to the Text: *All Kinds of Families* Review the book. Ask students to draw one type of "family" they saw in the book. Then have them complete the sentence to describe one way their objects are the same (e.g., *These objects are blue*).

COLLABORATE

Ask partners to share their drawings and read their sentences aloud. Then have them look at both drawings together. Ask: *Can you find a new way to sort all your objects?* See Teacher's Edition p. 720 for scaffolded support with this page.

ELD.PI.K.6.Em, ELD.PI.K.6.Ex, ELD.PI.K.6.Br; ELD.PI.K.10.Em
See the California Standards section

1.

new

smooth

curly

happy

2.

rough

sad

old

straight

COLLABORATE

Oral Vocabulary: Finding Opposites Read the adjectives as children echo-read. Talk about what the words mean. Then have children find pairs of pictures with opposite descriptions (e.g., *curly/straight*). Have them draw lines to connect the opposites.

Ask partners to read their opposites out loud: *new penny/old penny, rough ball/smooth ball, etc.* Then have them find opposites in the classroom (e.g., *a smooth blackboard/a rough piece of chalk*). See Teacher's Edition p. 724 for scaffolded support with this page.

(tl) Ken Cavanagh/McGraw-Hill Education; (tcl) Mark Steinmetz; (tcr) Iconotec/Glow Images; (tr) Fancy Collection/SuperStock; (bl) Creative Crop/Photodisc/Getty Images; (bcl) 2012 Ariel Alvarez/Flickr RF/Getty Images; (bcr) Ken Karp/McGraw-Hill Education; (br) Copyright © FoodCollection

ELD.PI.K.I.Em, ELD.PI.K.I.Ex, ELD.PI.K.I.Br See the California Standards section

1.

2.

3.

4.

Retell "We Come on Time" Review the story, then ask children to use the sequence of pictures to retell it. Ask questions such as: *How do Jan and Pete get to school? How do other children get to school?* Have students circle a way they get to school.

Ask partners to take turns retelling the story, using complete sentences. Then invite them to tell about their trip to school today. Encourage them to add details, and use complete sentences. See Teacher's Edition p. 726 for scaffolded support with this page.

ELD.PI.K.6.Em, ELD.PI.K.6.Ex, ELD.PI.K.6.Br; ELD.PI.K.I2a.Em, ELD.PI.K.I2a.Ex, ELD.PI.K.I2a.Br See the California Standards section

Writing Review "We Come on Time." Then, introduce the prompt: *How do the different ways you get to school help you make friends?* Have children draw one way to get to school, and write about how it could help them make friends.

ELD.PI.K.10.Em, ELD.PI.K.10.Ex; ELD.PI.K.11.Em
See the California Standards section

Have partners share their drawing and writing. Ask: Which way of getting to school is best for making friends? Offer the sentence frame: *I think _____ is best because _____.* See Teacher's Edition p. 727 for scaffolded support with this page.

Unit 10 • Week 2 • Writing **249**

She Did Dishes

Carla and her mom
had dinner and pie.
They used many dishes.
The stack was high.
Carla washed dishes.
She set them out to dry.
Then she asked for
a big slice of pie.

Grammar *Pronouns* Read the rhyme. Repeat, as children echo-read. Remind them that pronouns take the place of naming words. Read it again, tracking the words, asking children to clap for each pronoun. Have children underline pronouns and circle the nouns they replace.

Ask partners to write a sentence that has one or more names. Then have them rewrite the sentence, replacing the names with pronouns. See Teacher's Edition p. 733 for scaffolded support with this page.

ELD.PI.K.2.Em, ELD.PI.K.2.Ex; ELD.PI.K.5.Em, ELD.PI.K.5.Ex, ELD.PI.K.5.Br See the California Standards section

Where Does It Go?

Keep the fox with the fox.
Keep the cub with the cub.
Where does the bee go?
Keep the bee with the bee!
And where do I go?
You come with me!

fox

cub

bee

COLLABORATE

Fluency Read the rhyme. Then have children read it. Remind them to copy the intonation you use for questions and exclamations. Ask children to underline the high-frequency words *come* and *does* and *circle* words with the long *e* sound.

ELD.PI.K.5.Em, ELD.PI.K.5.Ex, ELD.PI.K.5.Br; ELD.PIII.K
See the California Standards section

Ask partners to take turns reading the rhyme to each other until they can read it fluently. Ask: *What are the children doing in the rhyme? Do you think they're friends? How do you know?* See Teacher's Edition p. 734 for scaffolded support with this page.

Weekly Concept: Protect Our Earth

? Essential Question

What ideas can you suggest to protect the environment?

Weekly Concept: Protect Our Earth Guide children to talk about the picture. Ask: *How are these people protecting the environment?* Have children circle the different ways people are protecting the environment.

COLLABORATE

Ask partners to share ideas for protecting the environment. Offer the sentence frame: *I can protect the environment by _____.* See Teacher's Edition p. 738 for scaffolded support with this page.

252 Unit 10 • Week 3 • Weekly Concept

ELD.PI.K.I.Em, ELD.PI.K.I.Ex, ELD.PI.K.I.Br See the California Standards section

1.

2.

3.

4.

Words and Categories: Helping Animals Guide children to describe the pictures. Explain that helping animals that live in the wild is one way to protect the environment. Have children draw one more way that people can care for animals in the empty box.

ELD.PI.K.I.Em, ELD.PI.K.I.Ex, ELD.PI.K.I.Br See the California Standards section

Ask partners to share their drawings and describe how their animals are being cared for. Then have children explain which animal they would most like to care for, and why. See Teacher's Edition p. 741 for scaffolded support with this page.

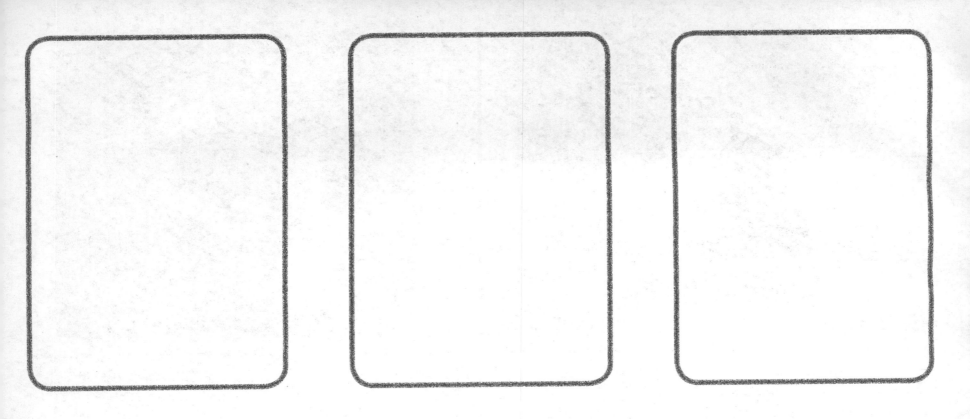

People help pandas by

Respond to the Text: *Panda Kindergarten* Review the book. Then ask children to draw three ways that people help the pandas. Have children complete the sentence with one way people help pandas.

Have partners use their drawings to help them retell the story. Then ask: *What did you learn about pandas from the book?* Children can share their answers with their partners. See Teacher's Edition p. 744 for scaffolded support with this page.

ELD.PI.K.6.Em, ELD.PI.K.6.Ex, ELD.PI.K.6.Br; ELD.PI.K.10.Em
See the California Standards section

Oral Vocabulary: Ways to Care for Earth Name the objects in the pictures. Say: *We can work with each of these objects to protect the environment. Can you explain how?* Have children draw another way they can protect the environment.

Ask partners to describe their drawings. Then have them take turns talking about each picture. Offer the sentence frame: *I can _____.* (E.g., *I can turn off the water; I can plant a tree,* etc.) See Teacher's Edition p. 748 for scaffolded support with this page.

1.

2.

3.

4.

Retell "Who Can Help?" Have children use the pictures to retell the story. Ask questions about each picture, such as: *What are the children doing? How are they helping the environment?*

Have partners takes turns describing the actions in the pictures using complete sentences: *The children are _____. This helps the environment because _____.* See Teacher's Edition p. 750 for scaffolded support with this page.

ELD.PI.K.6.Em, ELD.PI.K.6.Ex, ELD.PI.K.6.Br; ELD.PI.K.12a.Em, ELD.PI.K.12a.Ex, ELD.PI.K.12a.Br See the California Standards section

I help when I

_____

- -

_____

- -

_____ •

COLLABORATE

Writing Review "Who Can Help?" Introduce the writing prompt: _Look at the ideas in this selection. Then write a letter to a friend telling which ones you practice._ Guide children to draw one way they can help the environment, then complete the sentence.

ELD.PI.K.6.Em, ELD.PI.K.6.Ex; ELD.PI.K.10.Em, ELD.PI.K.10.Ex
See the California Standards section

Ask partners to describe their drawings and read their sentences aloud. Then ask: _What other ideas for helping were in the selection? Which ones do you practice?_ See Teacher's Edition p. 751 for scaffolded support with this page.

We Can, They Can

You and I can help.
We dig a hole.

Mom and Dad can help.
They plant a tree.

The tree can help.
It will make shade
for you and me.

Grammar: Pronouns Read the selection. Reread it, as children echo-read. Discuss the meaning of the selection, and any unfamiliar words. Then guide children to identify the pronouns and underline them.

Ask partners to take turns reading the selection as best they can. Have the other partner clap or snap each time they hear a pronoun. See Teacher's Edition p. 757 for scaffolded support with this page.

ELD.PI.K.5.Em, ELD.PI.K.5.Ex, ELD.PI.K.5.Br See the California Standards section

A Home for a Duck

Nate and Eve see a duck.
Where does a duck live?
What does it need?
They put the duck in a box.
They take it to a lake.
Now the duck can get wet.
That is a good home!

COLLABORATE

Fluency Read the selection with children. Have them read it again, copying your intonation and phrasing. Ask: *What do Nate and Eve find? Where do they take the duck?* Have children circle the words with long vowel sounds.

Ask partners to take turns reading the passage to each other until they can read it fluently. Ask them to demonstrate the way they read a sentence ending in an exclamation point. See Teacher's Edition p. 758 for scaffolded support with this page.

ELD.PI.K.5.Em, ELD.PI.K.5.Ex, ELD.PI.K.5.Br; ELD.PIII.K
See the California Standards section

The Alphabet

A: Apple – Stockdisc/PunchStock; B: Bat – CrackerClips/iStock/Getty Images Plus/Getty Images; C: Camel – Photokanok/ Stock/Getty Images Plus/Getty Images; D: Dolphin – imagebroker/Alamy; E: Egg – Pixtal/age footstock; F: Fire – Comstock Images/Alamy; G: Guitar – Jules Frazier/Photodisc/Getty Images; H: Hippo – subinpumsom/iStock/Getty Images Plus/Getty Images; I: Insect – Ingram Publishing/Fotosearch; J: Jump – Photodisc/Getty Images; K: Koala – ©Al Franklin/Corbis; L: Lemon – C Squared Studios/Photodisc/Getty Images; M: Map – McGraw-Hill Education; N: Nest – Siede Preis/Photodisc/Getty Images; O: Octopus – Photographers Choice RF/SuperStock; P: Piano – Ingram Publishing/Alamy; Q: Queen – Joshua Ets-Hokin/Photodisc/Getty Images; R: Rose – ranasu/iStock/Getty Images Plus/Getty Images; S: Sun – 97/E+/Getty Images; T: Turtle – Ingram Publishing; U: Umbrella – Stockbyte/Getty Images; V: Volcano – Westend61/Getty Images; W: Window – emarto/iStock/Getty Images Plus/Getty Images; X: Box – C Squared Studios/Photodisc/Getty Images; Y: Yo-Yo – D. Hurst/Alamy; Z: Zipper – Image State/Alamy

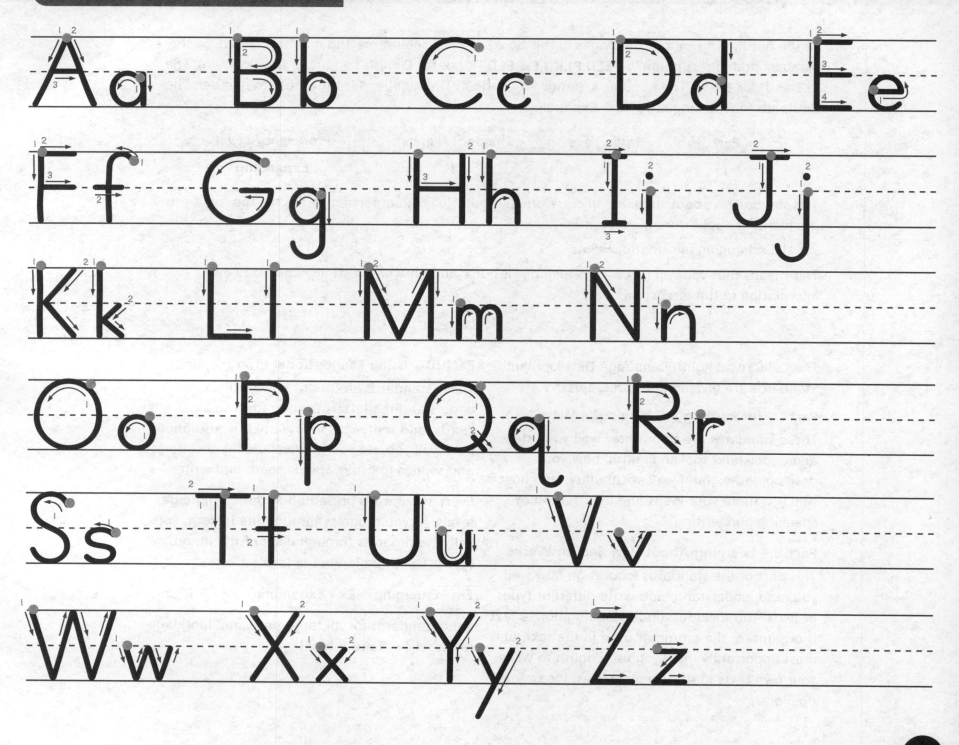

At the bottom of some of the pages in this book, you will see letters and numbers. What do these numbers and letters mean? In **ELD.PI.K.1.Ex, ELD** stands for English Language Development. The **PI** stands for Part I. The number **K** stands for Grade K. The number **1** is the standard number. The **Ex** stands for the language level Expanding.

Part	Grade Level	Standard Number	Proficiency Level
I	K	1	Expanding

This standard is about speaking in class, small groups, or with a partner to discuss the topic you are learning about during a lesson.

  1. Exchanging information/ideas

This means that you will follow turn-taking rules, ask and answer questions, and add new information to the discussion.

The California English Language Development Standards are divided into three parts:

Part I – Interacting in Meaningful Ways

These standards are about how well you listen and understand spoken English, how you develop and expand your vocabulary, and how well you share your ideas and information by speaking and writing.

Part II – Learning About How English Works

This part of the standards focuses on how well you read, understand, and write different types of texts. This includes: understanding how a text is organized, the grammar used in the text, and most importantly, how you use English to write your own texts to share your stories, ideas, and opinions.

Part III – Using Foundational Literacy Skills

These standards are about how well you understand the letters used to form sounds, words, and sentences in English. It is also about how well you use your understanding of letters and sounds to listen, speak, read, and write.

Every standard is presented in three language levels. As you progress through the lessons, you will also progress through each of the language levels. The three language levels are:

Em – Emerging   Ex – Expanding   Br – Bridging

Your Standards for all three parts and language levels follow. **Take a look!**

Grade K California English Language Development Standards

PART I: INTERACTING IN MEANINGFUL WAYS	
A. Collaborative	
1. Exchanging information and ideas	
PI.K.1.Em	Contribute to conversations and express ideas by asking and answering *yes-no* and *wh-* questions and responding using gestures, words, and simple phrases.
PI.K.1.Ex	Contribute to class, group, and partner discussions by listening attentively, following turn-taking rules, and asking and answering questions.
PI.K.1.Br	Contribute to class, group, and partner discussions by listening attentively, following turn-taking rules, and asking and answering questions.
2. Interacting via written English	
PI.K.2.Em	Collaborate with the teacher and peers on joint composing projects of short informational and literary texts that include minimal writing (labeling with a few words), using technology where appropriate for publishing, graphics, etc.
PI.K.2.Ex	Collaborate with the teacher and peers on joint composing projects of informational and literary texts that include some writing (e.g., short sentences), using technology where appropriate for publishing, graphics, etc.
PI.K.2.Br	Collaborate with the teacher and peers on joint composing projects of informational and literary texts that include a greater amount of writing (e.g., a very short story), using technology where appropriate for publishing, graphics, etc.
3. Offering opinions	
PI.K.3.Em	Offer opinions and ideas in conversations using a small set of learned phrases (e.g., *I think X.*), as well as open responses.
PI.K.3.Ex	Offer opinions in conversations using an expanded set of learned phrases (e.g., *I think/don't think X. I agree with X.*), as well as open responses, in order to gain and/or hold the floor.
PI.K.3.Br	Offer opinions in conversations using an expanded set of learned phrases (e.g., *I think/don't think X. I agree with X, but . . .*), as well as open responses, in order to gain and/or hold the floor or add information to an idea.
4. Adapting language choices	
PI.K.4.Em	No standard for kindergarten.
PI.K.4.Ex	No standard for kindergarten.
PI.K.4.Br	No standard for kindergarten.

Grade K California English Language Development Standards

B. Interpretive	
5. Listening actively	
PI.K.5.Em	Demonstrate active listening to read-alouds and oral presentations by asking and answering *yes-no* and *wh-* questions with oral sentence frames and substantial prompting and support.
PI.K.5.Ex	Demonstrate active listening to read-alouds and oral presentations by asking and answering questions with oral sentence frames and occasional prompting and support.
PI.K.5.Br	Demonstrate active listening to read-alouds and oral presentations by asking and answering detailed questions with minimal prompting and light support.
6. Reading/viewing closely	
PI.K.6.Em	Describe ideas, phenomena (e.g., parts of a plant), and text elements (e.g., characters) based on understanding of a select set of grade-level texts and viewing of multimedia with substantial support.
PI.K.6.Ex	Describe ideas, phenomena (e.g., how butterflies eat), and text elements- (e.g., setting, characters) in greater detail based on understanding of a variety of grade-level texts and viewing of multimedia with moderate support.
PI.K.6.Br	Describe ideas, phenomena (e.g., insect metamorphosis), and text elements (e.g., major events, characters, setting) using key details based on understanding of a variety of grade-level texts and viewing of multimedia with light support.
7. Evaluating language choices	
PI.K.7.Em	Describe the language an author uses to present an idea (e.g., the words and phrases used when a character is introduced) with prompting and substantial support.
PI.K.7.Ex	Describe the language an author uses to present an idea (e.g., the adjectives used to describe a character) with prompting and moderate support.
PI.K.7.Br	Describe the language an author uses to present or support an idea (e.g., the vocabulary used to describe people and places) with prompting and light support.
8. Analyzing language choice	
PI.K.8.Em	Distinguish how two different frequently used words (e.g., describing an action with the verb *walk* versus *run*) produce a different effect.
PI.K.8.Ex	Distinguish how two different words with similar meaning (e.g., describing an action as *walk* versus *march*) produce shades of meaning and a different effect.
PI.K.8.Br	Distinguish how multiple different words with similar meaning (e.g., walk, march, strut, prance) produce shades of meaning and a different effect.

Grade K California English Language Development Standards

C. Productive	
9. Presenting	
PI.K.9.Em	Plan and deliver very brief oral presentations (e.g., show and tell, describing a picture).
PI.K.9.Ex	Plan and deliver brief oral presentations on a variety of topics (e.g., show and tell, author's chair, recounting an experience, describing an animal).
PI.K.9.Br	Plan and deliver longer oral presentations on a variety of topics in a variety of content areas (e.g., retelling a story, describing a science experiment).
10. Composing/Writing	
PI.K.10.Em	Draw, dictate, and write to compose very short literary texts (e.g., story) and informational texts (e.g., a description of a dog), using familiar vocabulary collaboratively in shared language activities with an adult (e.g., joint construction of texts), with peers, and sometimes independently.
PI.K.10.Ex	Draw, dictate, and write to compose short literary texts (e.g., story) and informational texts (e.g., a description of dogs), collaboratively with an adult (e.g., joint construction of texts), with peers, and with increasing independence.
PI.K.10.Br	Draw, dictate, and write to compose longer literary texts (e.g., story) and informational texts (e.g., an information report on dogs), collaboratively with an adult (e.g., joint construction of texts), with peers, and independently using appropriate text organization.
11. Supporting opinions	
PI.K.11.Em	Offer opinions and provide good reasons (e.g., *My favorite book is X because X.*) referring to the text or to relevant background knowledge.
PI.K.11.Ex	Offer opinions and provide good reasons and some textual evidence or relevant background knowledge (e.g., paraphrased examples from text or knowledge of content).
PI.K.11.Br	Offer opinions and provide good reasons with detailed textual evidence or relevant background knowledge (e.g., specific examples from text or knowledge of content).

Grade K California English Language Development Standards

12. Selecting language resources

PI.K.12.Em	a) Retell texts and recount experiences using a select set of key words. b) Use a select number of general academic and domain-specific words to add detail (e.g., adding the word spicy to describe a favorite food, using the word larva when explaining insect metamorphosis) while speaking and composing.
PI.K.12.Ex	a) Retell texts and recount experiences using complete sentences and key words. b) Use a growing number of general academic and domain-specific words in order to add detail or to create shades of meaning (e.g., using the word scurry versus run) while speaking and composing.
PI.K.12.Br	a) Retell texts and recount experiences using increasingly detailed complete sentences and key words. b) Use a wide variety of general academic and domain-specific words, synonyms, antonyms, and non-literal language to create an effect (e.g., using the word suddenly to signal a change) or to create shades of meaning (e.g., The cat's fur was as white as snow.) while speaking and composing.

PART II: LEARNING ABOUT HOW ENGLISH WORKS

A. Structuring Cohesive Texts

1. Understanding text structure

PII.K.1.Em	Apply understanding of how text types are organized (e.g., how a story is organized by a sequence of events) to comprehending and composing texts in shared language activities guided by the teacher, with peers, and sometimes independently.
PII.K.1.Ex	Apply understanding of how different text types are organized to express ideas (e.g., how a story is organized sequentially with predictable stages versus how an informative text is organized by topic and details) to comprehending texts and composing texts in shared language activities guided by the teacher, collaboratively with peers, and with increasing independence.
PII.K.1.Br	Apply understanding of how different text types are organized predictably (e.g., a narrative text versus an informative text versus an opinion text) to comprehending texts and composing texts in shared language activities guided by the teacher, with peers, and independently.

2. Understanding cohesion

PII.K.2.Em	Apply basic understanding of how ideas, events, or reasons are linked throughout a text using more everyday connecting words or phrases (e.g., one time, then) to comprehending texts and composing texts in shared language activities guided by the teacher, with peers, and sometimes independently.

Grade K California English Language Development Standards

PII.K.2.Ex	Apply understanding of how ideas, events, or reasons are linked throughout a text using a growing number of connecting words or phrases (e.g., *next, after a long time*) to comprehending texts and composing texts in shared language activities guided by the teacher, collaboratively with peers, and with increasing independence.
PII.K.2.Br	Apply understanding of how ideas, events, or reasons are linked throughout a text using a variety of connecting words or phrases (e.g., *first/second/third, once, at the end*) to comprehending texts and composing texts in shared language activities guided by the teacher, with peers, and independently.

B. Expanding & Enriching Ideas

3. Using verbs and verb phrases

PII.K.3.Em	a) Use frequently used verbs (e.g., go, eat, run) and verb types (e.g., doing, saying, being/having, thinking/feeling) in shared language activities guided by the teacher and with increasing independence. b) Use simple verb tenses appropriate for the text type and discipline to convey time (e.g., simple past for recounting an experience) in shared language activities guided by the teacher and with increasing independence.
PII.K.3.Ex	a) Use a growing number of verbs and verb types (e.g., doing, saying, being/having, thinking/feeling) in shared language activities guided by the teacher and independently. b) Use a growing number of verb tenses appropriate for the text type and discipline to convey time (e.g., simple past tense for retelling, simple present for a science description) in shared language activities guided by the teacher and independently.
PII.K.3.Br	a) Use a wide variety of verbs and verb types (e.g., doing, saying, being/having, thinking/feeling) in shared language activities guided by the teacher and independently. b) Use a wide variety of verb tenses appropriate for the text type and discipline to convey time (e.g., simple present for a science description, simple future to predict) in shared language activities guided by the teacher and independently.

Grade K California English Language Development Standards

4. Using nouns and noun phrases	
PII.K.4.Em	Expand noun phrases in simple ways (e.g., adding a familiar adjective to describe a noun) in order to enrich the meaning of sentences and add details about ideas, people, things, etc., in shared language activities guided by the teacher and sometimes independently.
PII.K.4.Ex	Expand noun phrases in a growing number of ways (e.g., adding a newly learned adjective to a noun) in order to enrich the meaning of sentences and add details about ideas, people, things, etc., in shared language activities guided by the teacher and with increasing independence.
PII.K.4.Br	Expand noun phrases in a wide variety of ways (e.g., adding a variety of adjectives to noun phrases) in order to enrich the meaning of phrases/sentences and add details about ideas, people, things, etc., in shared language activities guided by the teacher and independently.
5. Modifying to add details	
PII.K.5.Em	Expand sentences with frequently used prepositional phrases (such as *in the house*, *on the boat*) to provide details (e.g., time, manner, place, cause) about a familiar activity or process in shared language activities guided by the teacher and sometimes independently.
PII.K.5.Ex	Expand sentences with prepositional phrases to provide details (e.g., time, manner, place, cause) about a familiar or new activity or process in shared language activities guided by the teacher and with increasing independence.
PII.K.5.Br	Expand simple and compound sentences with prepositional phrases to provide details (e.g., time, manner, place, cause) in shared language activities guided by the teacher and independently.
C. Connecting & Condensing Ideas	
6. Connecting ideas	
PII.K.6.Em	Combine clauses in a few basic ways to make connections between and join ideas (e.g., creating compound sentences using *and*, *but*, *so*) in shared language activities guided by the teacher and sometimes independently.
PII.K.6.Ex	Combine clauses in an increasing variety of ways to make connections between and join ideas, for example, to express cause/effect (e.g., *She jumped because the dog barked.*) in shared language activities guided by the teacher and with increasing independence.
PII.K.6.Br	Combine clauses in a wide variety of ways (e.g., rearranging complete simple sentences to form compound sentences) to make connections between and join ideas (e.g., *The boy was hungry. The boy ate a sandwich.* -> *The boy was hungry so he ate a sandwich.*) in shared language activities guided by the teacher and independently.

Grade K California English Language Development Standards

7. Condensing ideas	
PII.K.7.Em	No standard for kindergarten.
PII.K.7.Ex	No standard for kindergarten.
PII.K.7.Br	No standard for kindergarten.
PART III: FOUNDATIONAL LITERACY SKILLS (See Appendix A–Kindergarten):	
	Literacy in an Alphabetic Writing System • Print concepts • Phonological awareness • Phonics & word recognition • Fluency